Peace and Justice in the Scriptures of the World Religions:

Reflections on Non-Christian Scriptures

Denise Lardner Carmody
and
John Tully Carmody

PAULIST PRESS NEW YORK/MAHWAH

Book design by Kathleen Doyle.

Index prepared by Michael Kerrigan, C.S.P.

Copyright © 1988 by
Denise Carmody and John Carmody

Library of Congress Cataloging-in-Publication Data

Carmody, Denise Lardner, 1935–
    Peace and justice in the scriptures of the world religions :
  reflections on non-Christian scriptures / Denise Lardner Carmody,
  John Tully Carmody.
        p.   cm.
    Includes bibliographies.
    ISBN 0-8091-3014-9 (pbk.) : $8.95 (est.)
    1. Peace—Religious aspects.   2. Religion and justice.   3. Sacred
books.   I. Carmody, John, 1939–   II. Title.
BL65.P4C37 1988
291.1′7873—dc19   88-23416
                                                                   CIP

Published by Paulist Press
997 Macarthur Boulevard
Mahwah, New Jersey 07430

Printed and bound in the
United States of America

CONTENTS

For Karen and Ron Linhardt

PREFACE

The dialogues among Christians and adherents of other world religions now constitute a significant religious phenomenon. As communications have shrunk the world and economic, political, ecological, and military interdependencies have made the nations suspect their fates are linked, people interested in cross-cultural understanding have come to realize that interreligious dialogue is not a frill but a requisite. Among the results of such dialogue one can already number mutual criticism and rethinking concerning theological and philosophical foundations. Each partner to religious dialogue now must reckon with others who start from different premises, venerate different paradigmatic heroes, and expect different conclusions from a holy life. We leave to others the doctrinal changes likely to come from such reconsiderations. Our focus in this book is the perhaps more pressing matter of peace in a nuclear age and justice in a world with chasmic gaps between haves and have-nots.

We have chosen to focus on the scriptures of the non-Christian religions. Several considerations contributed to this choice. First, in all traditions the writings accounted scriptures hold pride of place and amount to classical expressions of what the tradition has thought most significant. Second, the scriptures comprise a span of writings from which one can easily obtain a representative sample for a college or adult education course, or even for a private study project. Third, we assume that most of our readers will come from a Christian background and so may find interesting forays into the writings that parallel the Old and New Testaments.

Our background is Christian, and no doubt this shows at many points. Nonetheless, we have taken a sympathetic, even admiring attitude toward each of the scriptures we treat, and we have both assumed and argued that something common runs through them all. This is the basic health or right order that one associates with what some have called the "perennial philosophy." Prior to modern Western culture, virtually all peoples revered a transcendent, divine reality and thought right relation to it the crux of human health, both individual and social. In dealing with texts from the scriptures of the world religions, we have stressed this perennial conviction and tried to make it bear on the strife and injustice of our own times. Naturally, we have not assumed that prior times were peaceful and just to a degree that made them qualitatively different from our own. But we have argued, sometimes implicitly and sometimes explicitly, that on the whole prior times had a better sense of right order, a perspective more interested in how things look under the aspect of eternity, than what one finds in present-day popular Western culture.

One wishing further study in the authors who have formed our own philosophy may consult the works of Eric Voegelin, Bernard Lonergan, Karl Rahner, and Michael Polanyi. Recent authors who have elicited our admiration for their blend of contemplative and political wisdom include Rosemary Haughton and Sebastian Moore. For further study in the scriptures of the world religions we recommend Kenneth Kramer, *World Scriptures: An Introduction to Comparative Religions* (New York: Paulist, 1986); *Sacred Texts of the World: A Universal Anthology,* ed. Ninian Smart and Richard D. Hecht (New York: Crossroad, 1982); and *The Holy Book in Comparative Perspective,* ed. Frederick M. Denny and Rodney L. Taylor (Columbia: University of South Carolina Press, 1985).

Chapter 1

INTRODUCTION

THE IMPERATIVE CALL TO PEACE AND JUSTICE

Inside the Christian churches, as inside the assemblies of all other religions, many people ponder the relation between their faith and the world they live in. Outside the religious assemblies, people on the streets of New York and New Delhi, San Francisco and Sao Paulo, ponder hunger, sickness, and warfare. For most religious faiths, loving God and attaining wisdom are manifested by loving fellow creatures and improving the world. To many of the contemporary world's five billion people, the problems of hunger, sickness, and warfare suggest the need for a new social order, a new worldview. In this book we assume that the resources Christianity might contribute to such a new social order and worldview are well known. If they are not, an hour's investigation could show one a year's worth of reading on the subject.[1]

Our focus is texts from the non-Christian religious traditions that suggest their resources for the conversions of mind and heart justice and peace require. In the last section of this chapter we offer a general orientation to the texts the book uses. Here let us linger with the notions of peace and justice, asking why it is that many people of good will now think "religion" and "God" carry an imperative call to forward both.

A line from an essay by Rosemary Haughton puts the answer in a nutshell: "It is in the giving and receiving of life and love that we discern the presence of God."[2] The context of the line is a reflection on the state of marriage nowadays. In the background stand Haughton's prior works on Catholic theology, including her brilliant book *The Passionate God,* which portray redemptive love breaking into history through human weakness and making God our fellow sufferer.[3] In the foreground stands Haughton's recent work in Gloucester, Massachusetts, with people down and out. Most of the people in her shelter are women and children, and many of them have been abused. Haughton has decried not only the systems that have fostered that abuse but the support such systems have drawn from patriarchal theology. As well, she has marveled at the good things that happen when the women share their stories and begin to pull together. The line we find so pregnant comes at the end of this reflection on sources of strength, encouragement, and renewal. It implies that love of other people and love of God often join into one experience, one salvific reality.

The late Karl Rahner (1904–1984), whom many commentators consider the most influential Catholic theologian of this century, spelled out this implication in a famous essay.[4] For him, too, God comes through history—the daily interactions that build people up and keep them going. Where there is charity and love, an old Christian song says, there is God (*Ubi charitas et amor, ibi Deus est*). Where there is peace and justice, faith seems warranted. Of course, we may only realize our profound need for peace, justice, love, and God when we suffer their lack. We may only come to grips with deeper aspects of human existence when the Stock Market crashes or a parent is diagnosed as having cancer. But even these negative, painful experiences bring the same lesson. God and ultimate meaning must be ingredient in daily life, in human work and affection, or they will not seem real. Conversely, without the depth, the ultimacy that God and religious wisdom signify, daily life will seem unworthy of the human spirit, may even seem a prison.

"Human work and affection" can conjure up genteel, refined images: architects at their drawing boards, parents swinging their kids. They can also conjure up peasants plodding home from a day of backbreaking work, women weeping in the *plaja major* for the children they have lost to butchery. Most of our world's five billion people do not live in genteel refinement. Much of nature now is in travail from environmental pollution. The countries that enjoy democratic politics and material prosperity are in the minority. The lives pockmarked by suffering predominate. In a great many situations, therefore, the giving and receiving of life and love follow patterns similar to Christ's cross. In a great many situations, the discernment of God is clouded, twisted, racked by pain. This does not mean God isn't discerned, the divine love isn't present. It does mean that what Jesus called "The Reign of God" remains far from fully realized.

Realizing peace and justice among human beings would be tantamount to realizing the Reign of God. To be sure, union with God implies more than peace and justice among human beings, is richer. But Christianity is an incarnational religion. It thinks the Word of God took flesh and dwelt among us. Therefore, it thinks how we treat one another is crucially important. To have worldly goods and close one's heart to another person in need is to make a mockery of professing to love God (I John 3:17). To abuse creation, not see that water and oil are sacramental, is to render faith inoperative, even bogus.

From Christian instinct, therefore, comes a call to treat the world (nature and other people) as the place where one's faith will be realized. Just as Jesus could be known by the signs he gave, the works he performed, so his followers can be known by what they do, how they live. The same holds for people who don't profess to follow Jesus, whether they are religious or irreligious. The great leveler is what we do, how we live. Our words, even our ideals, are less trustworthy. Similarly, a society can be known by where it puts its money, how its work and wealth are disbursed. If the needs of the many are more important than the wants of the few, a society is genuinely democratic. If children, women, people of color, or people who are religious, cultural, or sexual minorities fare badly, a society in fact is ungodly, needs reform.

These theses would hold in any time, apply on any continent. Nowadays, however, we live in societies that increasingly become more interrelated. Financially, the markets of Japan, Hong Kong, Europe, and the United States often seem to be but subsets of a single global economy. Ecologically, the pollution of one country travels to the air, the water, the land of many others. And even culturally, in the realm of ideas, national boundaries can seem fictitious. Certainly scientists and artists communicate across languages and different heritages. Certainly the Nobel prizes address the whole world.

Slowly but surely, a similar interrelation is appearing among the religions, as we see in the next section. There are internal pressures promoting interreligious dialogue (for example, the desire to relate one's own faith to that of others who once seemed far away but now are global neighbors), but equally significant are the common social problems the nations experience.

Which brings us back to the call to peace and justice. Whether we look at the high road of scientific exchange, cultural enrichment, and religious dialogue, or the low road of nuclear arms, ecological pollution, and massive poverty, peace (getting along, minimizing hostilities) and justice (sharing fairly, minimizing the causes of hostilities) seem imperative. The only road we reasonably can travel, the only way forward, the only viable option is to promote cooperation, understanding, mutual respect, mutual concern—all the virtues that sound like platitudes until one analyzes what has to happen if we are not to blow our one world up.

We are not the first generation to realize the need for peace and justice, of course, but in our time the need is more imperative, because for the first time planetary destruction is a real possibility. The world has more people than ever before, and more suffering. The ecosystems have never been so threatened. Our century has witnessed the largest massacres recorded in history. Due to greatly increased communications, aspirations have never been higher, and so people have seldom been so aware things ought to be very different. If all of this does not mount an imperative call to peace and justice, conscience has no relation to history.

CONTEMPORARY INTERRELIGIOUS DIALOGUE

On several fronts, people of religious faith are now talking across traditions. Realizing that full understanding is a long way off, and may require a pyschological sophistication presently beyond most believers, they usually content themselves with establishing an atmosphere in which all partners might feel free to listen without feeling threatened and to speak with full honesty. Thus, one now finds journals for ecumenical studies and such specialized topics as Buddhist-Christian dialogue.[4a] One finds books in which Jews, Christians and Muslims discuss social justice and books in which Muslims and Christians discuss their understandings of God.[5] Legion are the studies that compare traditions, and recently Christian theologians have started to approach such studies as having intrinsic, more than accidental bearing on their own work of understanding Jesus and the gospel.[6] As mentioned, some of the stimulus to this interreligious discussion comes from the desire simply to understand people who used to seem distant foreigners but now are fellow citizens of an increasingly unitary world. Some also comes from the awareness that questions of world peace and international justice cloud all horizons, and that if the world's religious traditions don't bring their repositories of wisdom to bear on such questions they may have the blood of hundreds of millions on their heads.

Not to put too fine a point on it, our prejudice is that the detached, academic aspects of interreligious dialogue deserve full support but that the more pressing need is for personal, involved, existential exchanges. Until people of different faiths feel they are fully equal in their humanity and so all have things to teach and things to learn, the anthropological foundations of effective dialogue will still be missing. Until people of different faiths feel God has addressed them all and so all have religious wisdom to teach and religious wisdom to learn, the theological foundations of effective dialogue will still be missing. And the only way to build either of these foundations is to reveal where one really lives, how one actually suffers, what one's "faith" in fact means for making it through the day and being able to bless the Master of the Universe or the Wisdom that has Gone Beyond.

Further, we are not likely to bring ultimate, truly religious perspectives to bear on problems of achieving peace and justice until we are addressing them from the heart, where the realest parts of ourselves lodge, our best love and insight. Academic discussions, for all their value, usually are too removed from the heart of the religious matter to generate the creativity and passion effective work for peace and justice requires. Something more personal (although equally disciplined and intelligent); something more confessional (although equally hard on self-indulgence); something frankly mystical (in the sense of immersed in the fullness of ultimate reality, longing to feel the love of God)—this is the only sort of dialogue that might help us muster the energy to remake our shattered world.

Our own prejudices therefore are out on the table, and from them come the goal of this book. We have hoped to produce reflections useful in a variety of college courses and adult discussion groups, and so we accept the responsibility of explaining the background that the various world-religious scriptures we are using assume. But our ambition goes beyond providing information. Foolish as it may be, we hope to get inside the texts we use sufficiently to glimpse the love of God and life they stemmed from and traditionally have been honored for arousing, because it is this inside dimension, this esoteric pulse, that holds the most promise of revealing how Hinduism or Buddhism, Confucianism or Taoism, Judaism or Islam would instruct us about attaining peace and justice.

In making such an interior dialogue our ambition, we are not denying the significance of the externals of the world religions. Their histories, rituals, diversities of doctrinal schools, ethical traditions, and the like certainly have fashioned much of their realities. What one might call the exoteric, pluralistic side of any religious tradition deserves full study, and any comprehensive approach to the question of what the religions have to offer for achieving peace and justice certainly would have to deal with them. But ours is not a comprehensive study. In other places we have dealt with the full range of data the world religions present, as well as with their overall ethical traditions.[7] Here we are interested in something more limited and more intense. Here we are after the passion of the religion, the vision that makes people love Krishna, love the Buddha, revere Confucius or Lao Tzu with all their heart. Here we want to follow the echoes of the Jews who for centuries loved Torah to tears and with joy thought it near, available, possible; to follow Muslims who trembled when the muzzein announced the call to prayer and thrilled to the recitals given to Muhammad.

Is it possible for an outsider to approach such inner sanctums? Can one ever replicate the love that has formed the psyches of people who believe differently, ever take to heart the words that have been their vademecums, their last resources in the darkest night? Perhaps not, but our times require us to try. Because unless we do replicate at least stirrings of the love that has energized Muslims and Buddhists, Jews and Confucians, we won't feel how they can be our collaborators, people with whom we might reconstitute our broken world. Unless what has consoled them in the darkest night becomes consoling to us, the prospect of nuclear winter will become for all of us both more real and less bearable.

To be sure, one ought to be modest about the practical consequences any work for conversion is likely to produce. We plant, others water, but only God gives the increase. And what one can communicate in a book, through images and concepts, is never more than propaedeutical—the beginning, preliminary stuff on which real education, real change of minds and hearts, might build. Moreover, if Marxism and liberation theology have taught us anything it should be the primacy of praxis. We won't even know what "peace" and "justice" denote until we have suffered for them, have put our bodies and minds on the line. So despite the hot rhetoric, we realize we should stay cool when speaking of the effects our reflections might work. Even though the imagination leaps ahead to the changes intellectual visions and conversions might empower, good judgment intervenes to remind us that massive problems remain. Indeed, the obstacles to peace and justice, both at home and abroad, are such that speaking of miracles is no hyperbole. If we are to avoid Armageddon and ecological disaster, God will have to manage history so it veers away from the probabilities growing in our current policies.

Still, each of us can only do, and must in conscience try to do, what our talents and circumstances allow. We have spent some time with the scriptures of the great world religions. For years we have tried to mediate their wisdom to students in our classrooms, to mainly anonymous readers of our books. So maybe we can contribute some light, some prodding, some perspective on what the great religious books suggest. If this helps, our time will have been justified. If it doesn't help, turns out to be another feckless venture, at least we will have a thin defense to hold between us and the Master asking how we have used our talents.

It's a strange equipoise, a delicate balance, that the religious wisdoms would inculcate, but its gist echoes in the prayer composed by Reinhold Niebuhr and popularized by Alcoholics Anonymous—the prayer for the grace to change the things one can, to accept the things one can't, and to have the wisdom to know the difference. At the moment, we don't have this wisdom. We have never tried to storm the citadels of the religious scriptures and come away with the love that makes their people holy. The image of the Israelites despoiling the Egyptians comes to mind, but we must reject that as pertaining to divisions we can no longer afford. Today the Bhagavad-Gita, the Dhammapada, the Analects, the Tao Te Ching, the Talmud, and the Qur'an have to become the property of all people, as does the New Testament. Today we can't afford the luxury of despoiling one another and so making enemies. We have to enter with such humility, as well as such passionate desire, that it is clear we want only to learn and realize full well the limits of outsiders' insights. Nonetheless, we also have to insist on the sameness of human needs and human hopes, the equality of people in their hunger for justice and peace, and so assert the capacity all people have for understanding a religious classic.

AN ORIENTATION

The format of this book is commentary on selections from six religious "scriptures" (the term believers are apt to use) or "classics" (the term humanistic outsiders might use).[8] A religious or sacred scripture is a writing thought to reveal the holy God or ultimate reality. A classic is a writing in which all later generations can estimate their humanity, as in a mirror. For our purposes, the differences between these terms, and their overlappings, don't matter very much. The Bhagavad-Gita is both a Hindu scripture (less officially so than the Vedas, but in practice treated as such) and a classic that has given many non-Hindus much light. The Dhammapada is part of the Buddhist canon (list of officially approved writings) but also a work many non-Buddhists have loved for its insights, its instruction in the psychology of the moral life. The same with the Analects, the Tao Te Ching, the Talmud (not on the same scriptural level as the Hebrew Bible, but a continuance of Torah [divine instruction]) and the Qur'an. Perhaps three billion people in our world now adhere to traditions venerating these works as privileged guidance—which leaves two billion who ideally would be open to their message, if only because they thought sixty percent of their fellows too large a fraction to ignore.

We are not saying, of course, that all Hindus are shaped, let alone determined, by the Bhagavad-Gita. We are not assuming that the Dhammapada is a complete capsule of Buddhism. It is probably impossible to determine how much the Confucian classics now influence (proximately or remotely) the more than one billion Chinese. The Tao Te Ching may be more honored in the West (it is the most translated Eastern text) than in lands where the Tao traditionally held sway. Many reformed and secular Jews have put aside the Talmud, while the Qur'an can seem such an insiders' book that its import for people not living in a Muslim theocracy can seem negligible.

Admitting these qualifications, and many others that legitimately might be made, we still think the venture of probing other people's scriptures for their universal import worth attempting. The Bhagavad-Gita doesn't have to shape all 700 million Hindus for us to find it instructive about peace and justice, any more than the New Testament has to rule in all one billion hearts extrinsically denominated "Christian." Indeed, present-day literary theory is eloquent about the independence of a text, the ways in which it stands free of its author, original context, and interpretational history. A text can speak afresh to any new reader. In our opinion that reader is foolish to disregard the author's probable intentions and the traditional interpretations the text has received. Equally, however, readers should feel free to take a text to heart and let it shed what light, generate what warmth, it would. Cardinal Newman's motto, *cor ad cor loquitur* ("heart speaks to heart") applies to reading as well as to face-to-face conversations. The Cardinal was an astute observer of religious understanding, as his influential *A Grammar of Assent* reveals. Using his motto, we can remind ourselves that understanding, interpretation, employs the imagination and the affections as much as the intellect. Indeed, in the measure understanding has the potential for changing lives, initiating significant actions, it is holistic—reminiscent of the Bible's ideal for the love of God: with whole mind, heart, soul, and strength. So we would be the last people in the world to discourage students from taking these texts to heart, worrying them like bones whose marrow might be just what the system needed. The more fully students engage with these texts, challenge the terms the texts provide, chew over our interpretations, and open themselves to being judged by the texts in turn, the richer will be the yield and education.

It is a tired ploy to pound on the etymology of "education" and note that the enterprise ought to be leading students out to something, or liberating something in students that hitherto they hadn't realized they had or could be. Nonetheless, we cannot resist adding a tap of our own. The scriptures, the classics, are the premier texts of liberation. Minimally, they tend to free hearers from the narrowness, the lack of vision, that has kept their humanity shrunken. In the best of cases, they break open the full range of possibility human nature portends, showing hearers how different their selves, their societies, their God might be, were their spirits fed by better images. The limits of our worlds, our selves, are the images we can draw upon, the possibilities we can think and feel. If we can imagine a Kingdom of Heaven, despotic regimes on earth will be cut down to size. The Dhammapada is quite right: we are what we think. The Jewish and Christian scriptures are on the mark: faith is the measure.

What we think and believe of course does not automatically change the world. To dream of peace and justice is one thing, to produce the structural changes that will enfranchise more people, heal more sickly children, whittle down nuclear arsenals, generate land reform, clean up the skies and the oceans is quite another. And yet in practice both ideals and achievements seem to develop dialectically, by the clash of thought and experience, imagination and trial and error. One sees a grand possibility, a way to become more human, and gives it a try. Limping, bruised but wiser, one goes back to the monastery, the prie-dieu, the Taoist retirement and thinks again. Eventually a rhythm of doing and assessing, venturing and praying, starts to take hold, mimicking the intake and output of one's breathing.

The assumption and sales pitch of people who promote the scriptures and classics is that they ought to stand high on the list of what we take in, what we use for nourishment. How they will put out energy and direction remains to be seen and historically has been quite varied. Just as there is no single prescription for what Christians will make of the Pauline writ of emancipation ("for freedom Christ has set us free" [Gal. 5:1]), so there is no single prescription for what monks or laypeople are likely to do with the Dhammapada's insights about the significance of what one thinks. There is great agreement among readers of the classics, however, that interacting with them has brought transcendence—movement beyond one's prior sense of self and boundaries, movement out to the mystery of God. Thus Bernard Lonergan, one of the most powerful Catholic minds of this century, was challenged and invigorated by studying Thomas Aquinas, as Karl Rahner had been. Karl Barth, a giant of twentieth century Protestant thought, grew by wrestling with Paul's epistle to the Romans (and wrestling against Nazi ideology). Mahatma Gandhi loved the Bhagavad-Gita and the New Testament. Elie Wiesel, the Jewish Nobel peace laureate, was nourished by the Bible, the Talmud, the Hasidic masters, and the Kabbala. So at times the Dhammapada might be paraphrased as "we are what we read, what we meditate upon." If we fill our minds with pictures of Jesus and Muhammad, Confucius and the Buddha, Krishna and the Baal

Shem Tov, we will dwell on noble images, feel challenged by holy emotions. If we add pictures of Mary and the Magdalene, Fatima and Rab'ia, Esther and Deborah, we will have the necessary feminine complements. The scriptures are written for our instruction and nourishment. We should use them as personally and freely as good sense and good conscience allow. In the measure they point to peace and justice, we should hail them as words for our time (and so as words of eternal life). So let us expect great things of them, hoping that they can in fact lay out the path that is straight, the path that leads to a world fit to live in.

Discussion Questions

1. How does peace relate to images of God?
2. How does justice relate to human wisdom?
3. Why has interreligious dialogue recently come alive?
4. What makes understanding one another's scriptures possible?
5. What images dominate contemporary Western views of international justice?
6. What do images of Mary and the Magdalene add to images of Jesus and Paul?

Notes

1. Orbis publishing company has an extensive line of works on liberation theology. Representative Christian authors are the Catholic Gustavo Gutierrez and the Protestant Robert McAfee Brown. Our own contributions include *The Quiet Imperative* and *Like an Ever-Flowing Stream* (Nashville: The Upper Room, 1986, 1987).

2. Rosemary Haughton, "Marriage in Women's New

Consciousness," in *Commitment to Partnership: Explorations of the Theology of Marriage,* ed. William P. Roberts (New York: Paulist, 1987), p. 151.

3. Rosemary Haughton, *The Passionate God* (New York: Paulist, 1981).

4. See *Journal of Ecumenical Studies,* ed. Leonard Swidler (Philadelphia: Temple University) and *Buddhist-Christian Studies,* ed. David W. Chappell (Honolulu: University of Hawaii).

4a. Karl Rahner, "Reflections on the Unity of the Love of Neighbor and the Love of God," in *Theological Investigations,* 6 (Baltimore: Helicon, 1969), pp. 231–249.

5. See *World Faiths and the New World Order,* ed. Joseph Gremillion and William Ryan (Washington: The Interreligious Peace Colloquium, 1978), and *We Believe in One God,* ed. Annemarie Schimmel and Abdoldjavad Falaturi (New York: Seabury, 1979).

6. See F.E. Peters, *Children of Abraham* (Princeton, N.J.: Princeton University Press, 1981), Paul F. Knitter, *No Other Name?* (Maryknoll, N.Y.: Orbis, 1985), Hans Küng *et al., Christianity and the World Religions* (Garden City, N.Y.: Doubleday, 1986).

7. Denise Lardner Carmody and John Tully Carmody, *Ways to the Center,* 3rd ed. (Belmont, Calif: Wadsworth, 1989), *The Story of World Religions* (Mountain View, Calif.: Mayfield, 1988), *How To Live Well: Ethics in the World Religions* (Belmont, Calif: Wadsworth, 1987).

8. See *The Holy Book in Comparative Perspective,* ed. Frederick M. Denny and Rodney L. Taylor (Columbia: University of South Carolina Press, 1985), and David Tracy, *The Analogical Imagination* (New York: Crossroad, 1981).

Chapter 2

HINDUISM AND THE BHAGAVAD-GITA

THE HINDU WORLDVIEW

"Hinduism" is, to say the least, an imprecise term. Although we regularly see it occurring in a list of world religions, alongside Christianity, Judaism, Islam, Buddhism, and other traditions, it is as much many religions as one.[1] Perhaps we could say the same about Christianity, insofar as Protestantism, Orthodoxy, and Catholicism denominate three different traditions (and within them national, ethnic, and sectarian differences add further variety). Still, Christianity has long held that the Church, the community of believers, must be one. Indeed, unity is the first of the four marks long associated with the Church: one, holy, catholic, and apostolic. Hinduism has no such bone-deep longing for unity.

In many ways, Hinduism is the national culture of the Indian sub-continent. Forged by the union of the cultures of Aryan invaders who swept in from the Northwest around 2000-1500 B.C.E. (Before the Common Era = B.C.) and aboriginal Indian peoples, it mixes reverence of fertility and the forces of nature with yoga, theistic devotion to high gods such as Krishna (an avatar or manifestation-form of Vishnu) and Shiva, worship of mother goddesses, and other religious expressions. However, if one is willing to risk a few abstractions, certain notions seem to cut across the entire Hindu cultural complex.

One is the notion of karma, which perhaps is best understood as a moral law of cause and effect. We act in the present according to what we have become through the past, and how we act in the present shapes what we shall be in the future. For example, if we have been lazy and undisciplined, it should come as no surprise that we are ill-equipped to face a crisis demanding energy and self-control. Similarly, if today we put off what can wait until tomorrow, we should not be surprised to discover that the day after tomorrow finds the task still undone. Most Hindus accept karma as an indication, if not an explanation, of why people are what they are and do what they do. Pressed too far, the doctrine of karma would seem to eliminate human freedom: I am what I am (the philosophy of Popeye) so don't expect me to change. Yet few Hindus in practice haven't held other people and themselves responsible for the crimes, and the good deeds, they have committed. Few in practice haven't affirmed human responsibility and so human freedom. Nonetheless, the belief in karma has made Hindus quite tolerant of the imperfections in human society, all the more so when they have imagined the world to be eternal (expanding and contracting through measureless ages [kalpas]) and human beings to be destined for many lives (reincarnation).

The concept that has kept karma from being like a sentence to a prison where the main work would be walking a treadmill is moksha. It signifies release and freedom from the world dominated by karma and reincarnation. Moksha says there is a state where karma doesn't hold, where existence is not conditioned by the past. And there is a way to this state, this share in the existence enjoyed by the ultimate reality, the Brahman that is the inmost being of all things. The way is detachment, becoming desireless. When one does not desire, is indifferent to pleasure and pain, success and failure, karma has nothing to grasp. Desire is the toehold ignorant people offer karma, the place where it can sink in its talons. When one has become fully purified of desire, the inertia that keeps one in the cycle of death and rebirth (called samsara) evanesces.

Then one escapes to the being, bliss, and full awareness of divine, ultimate reality. Then change and time are no more. Moksha is the Hindu equivalent of the Christian heaven (the Hindu "heavens" and "hells" are intermediate and passing states, and so are not equivalent to the Christian heaven and hell, which are definitive). It is the highest goal in life (pleasure, wealth, and duty are lower but still legitimate goals) and the objective of the Hindu saints.

Dharma, which translates as both "Teaching" and "duty," is another important Hindu concept. As Teaching, it derives from the visions of the holy seers whose wisdom is expressed in the Vedas, the holiest Hindu scriptures. Dharma summarizes the Aryan traditions, gives the obligations of the main castes comprising Indian society (priests, warriors, farmers/tradespeople, and workers), and lays out the sanctioned paths to moksha. Foremost among these paths are the meditational way of the yogin, the way of intellectual vision, the way of pure (desireless) work, and the way of devotion (bhakti). This last, bhakti, has been the most popular Hindu pathway. The millions who have revered a god such as Krishna or Shiva, a goddess such as Kali or the Mahadevi (Great Goddess), have tried to bind themselves to the deity (who lives on the far side of karma, in the realm of moksha and salvation) through ardent, even erotic love. Yoga entailed leisure and great discipline of both body and mind. Intellectual penetration of Dharma demanded schooling, leisure, and long study. Even to purify one's work, cleanse one's action of desire, seemed beyond the common person. But love—who had not felt its yearning, not longed for its consummation? So love became the most popular religious pathway, and the bhakta (devotee of a god or goddess) became the prevalent religious type.

This background provides some context for the Bhagavad-Gita. The Gita is an eclectic, catholic work, which no doubt has contributed to its usefulness and popularity. It has something for everyone: people who want revelations of the divine splendor, people interested in the problem of action, people concerned about warfare and killing (as epitomes of evil), people interested in yoga, people wanting to approach the deity in love. The literary context of the Bhagavad-Gita is an extended poem, called the Mahabharata, about a great war that took place in prehistoric times. On the frame of this war the Hindu poets, philosophers, and meditation masters who contributed at least raw materials have strung edifying stories, ethical analyses, myths, comic entertainments, and much more. The Mahabharata, like Hinduism itself, is more an inclusive museum than an exclusive treatise or religious work. It throws nothing away. So, many of its parts sit alongside other parts quite awkwardly, seeming to produce contradictions. Yet the typical Hindu finds not contradiction but complement. Each part, each insight, each point of view has its truth. The whole of Truth or Reality will always escape us, but the more angles we incorporate the closer we will come. So Hinduism is doctrinally tolerant (even though individual Indians may be quite intolerant and polemical, as witness the religious hatreds that divide Hindus, Muslims, and Sikhs to this day). It is a tradition of both/and rather than either/or.

The Gita exemplifies this tolerance and complexity, but not to the point of losing all focus. In the beginning Arjuna, a young warrior, puts to Krishna the question whether he should fight in what promises to be a bloody internecine war. This question leads to many side alleys and back streets, but the Gita never strays too far from the import of Arjuna's dilemma: How should one understand the self? For what should one live? How can one gain full freedom and realism, pleasing the deity?

Insofar as the answers to these questions compose something unified, the spirituality of the self seems the key. Krishna teaches Arjuna that the realest part of any person is imperishable. What happens to the body is less important than what happens to the soul, because the body is bound to perish while the soul will continue to exist with the maimings, or the rectitudes, it has achieved. So the great task is to purify the self, liberate it from gross desires, and develop its strengths through meditation and study (exercises that facilitate understanding the true proportions of reality). Sustaining the self in its labors, which can be arduous, is the love of Krishna himself. In chapter 18 of the Gita comes the paramount revelation: the devotee is dear to the deity. Clinging to this assurance, the devotee need fear none of the labors or pains the path can entail.

1:28–29: WAR

" 'O Krishna, when I see my own people ranged, drawn near, impatient to give battle, my limbs cannot hold me and my mouth becomes dry, and trembling shakes my whole body. My hair all stands on end.' "[2]

The speaker is Arjuna, giving vent to the horror and despair welling up in his heart. Krishna to this point is more a valet than a god revealed to possess heavenly power and splendor (as later he will be). Arjuna is contemplating the battle about to unfold. It will pit members of the same family against one another, bringing cousin to slay cousin and friend to slay friend. No doubt fear plays some part in what Arjuna feels, but more central is dread. The entire venture seems so senseless that his spirit flags, his knees go weak. What good-to-be-gained could possibly outweigh the slaughter this war will entail? What joy will the victors, their women and children, feel that will compensate for their losses, let alone for the losses of the defeated? Arjuna is ready to chuck the whole thing over, turn in his warrior's shield. As few other places in religious scripture, these lines in the Bhagavad-Gita display the depression the prospect of war should inflict. In contrast to the enthusiasm, the animal zeal war is supposed to arouse in military types, if not in "real men" everywhere, Arjuna's depression speaks of deeper things.

One might say that women typically have felt these deeper things and so regularly have been revolted by war. Across their mind's eye have passed the bodies sure to be carted home, the mangled limbs sure to need suturing. To be sure, a few women stand out as redoubtable warriors, for example, the biblical Deborah and Jael (Judges 4–5). And Hinduism is more prone to put destructiveness in the deity, female and male, than Western religions have been, as the function of Shiva as the Destroyer testifies. For Hinduism life and death, creation and destruction, are equal parts of the cosmic process. Both are necessary in the world we have, so both must be accepted. Thus a leading female Hindu deity, Kali, tends to have a devouring, blood-lusty aspect. Sometimes she is a welcoming mother, but other times she wears a garland of skulls and has a maw dripping with blood (in which aspect she can stand for Time, which eventually consumes everything).

Granted these qualifications, however, and trying to draw from the reaction of Arjuna the insights most helpful for promoting peace and justice today, we do well to ponder the depression, the revulsion, the text describes. If it is the reaction of a healthy spirit, the sort of response sane people everywhere would make, it displays warfare as an inhuman, unacceptable option. Like sin, which often it manifests, warfare would be intrinsically irrational. Examining its core, one would find nothing for the mind to grasp, nothing for the heart to love. Sin is precisely the mystery of iniquity, the boggle that people would do what is to no one's real benefit. War is precisely the mystery of the human need to dominate, retaliate, inflict hurt, risk destruction out of all proportion to the benefits that might accrue.

Obviously, history has been peppered with wars, as the individual lives of human beings have been peppered with sins. The irrational is never on holiday. But the fact that wars and sins occur does not justify their existence, any more than the fact that they are irrational justifies our ignoring them.

What we have to contend with is the prevalence of their enormity, the inordinate attraction they have held for so many. If Arjuna's is the response of health, indeed of common sense, why are so many people diseased? How does warfare work its wiles?

In Hindu terms, as we suggested, the source of most evils is desire. True enough, later the Gita will justify warfare, Krishna telling Arjuna that it is better for him to fulfill the responsibilities of his warrior caste than to abdicate them for the pacificism proper to priests. Krishna's argument then will be that there is no ultimate slaying and being slain, because only bodies perish. The core of the personality, the spirit, is imperishable. Nonetheless, Hinduism always opposed this defense of warfare, as it opposed *himsa* (hurting, aggression) generally, as inimical to holiness or the pursuit of moksha. In warfare it has seen desire swollen large, lust for material gain and inflicting hurt chaining thousands more tightly to the cycle of births and deaths.

Still, as we have noted, the Hindu tradition often speaks out of both sides of its mouth and does not think consistency the highest of virtues. In effect, it has wanted to have it both ways, both condemning warfare and justifying or accepting certain particular wars. Christianity has done much the same, embracing both a pacificist strain, that has much warrant in the words and example of Jesus, and a strain that thinks defense of the innocent against unjust aggression a religious responsibility. The just war theory that developed out of this second position had so many and such stringent conditions attached that many observers have concluded that, historically, a just war is hard to find. Moreover, with the advent of nuclear weapons the case for a just war is even harder to make (many, in fact, would say it is impossible). If the scenario for nuclear winter be accepted, so that significant explosion of nuclear weapons would probably result in the destruction of the ecosphere, nuclear war becomes matricide: killing the mother earth from whom all life has sprung.

Certainly the Gita, written perhaps 2300 years ago, had no prospects of nuclear winter in mind. Arjuna is mainly revolted by the prospect of killing relatives, people he has loved in the bosom of his extended family. But this instinct can be sharpened, broadened, deepened. If "relatives" were to name all people who shared one's human nature, all warfare would be family tragedy. If the environment were included in those assaulted by modern warfare, modern warfare would approach ecocide, matricide. Finally, there is the question that deeper religious instinct would have put at the outset: How does warfare stand in the eyes of the divinity? What does God think, say, feel about human slaughter?

This is not so simple a question as Christian pacifists sometimes suggest, because there are many gods in world history and the observation of Xenophanes that most of them are made in the image of the people petitioning them is on the mark. As he said, if horses served gods those gods undoubtedly would be in the form of horses. Similarly, the gods warrior peoples (like the Aryans) have worshipped unsurprisingly themselves have been heavenly battlers. Indra, for example, one of the leading gods of the Vedas, was not only the god of the storm but a lusty warrior who loved combat and drinking songs. The God of the Hebrew Bible on the whole is compassionate, merciful, slow to anger and abounding in steadfast love, but more than traces of his warrior predecessor remain. Thus the God who leads the Israelites out of Egypt and presides over their conquest of a Canaanite territory of their own is the leader of their army, the general of their forces. The German soldiers of World War II who had "God with us" on their belt-buckles could appeal to this biblical tradition, as some Muslim fighters of our day glorify their slaughtering as *Jihad*—struggle against the ungodly.

Once again, though, we suggest a choice against these martial theologies, a choice for the instinct displayed when Arjuna is revolted. Bracketing for a while the question of how to respond to evil that has its fangs bared and is seeking one's throat, we want to linger with Arjuna's state of soul, thinking it not womanish or overly delicate but profoundly religious. No genuine God, in our view, positively desires warfare. The combat of Jesus against Satan is a poor warrant for painting his Father as one who sanctions human slaughter, as it is a poor warrant for arguing that Jesus' disciples, or any people of sound mind, should think human combat business as usual. The God who creates out of love, and saves out of love, must be one with Arjuna in groaning at the prospect of another spasm of hatred and destruction. The people who equate the wastage of war with the price of real manhood (let alone the price of biblical faith) know little about this Creator. In their foolishness, their unconversion, they would make God as de-mon-driven and carnal as themselves. The Gita, like the New Testament, suggests that the true divinity is spiritual—not in the sense of ethereal, inhuman, but in the sense of too reason-able, good, and creative to get dead-ended into approving people's mutual maiming. Warfare is a confession that our hu-manity has failed. It is a counsel of despair, as Arjuna heard it to be. If we would be human, we have to place warfare atop the list of the fallacies, the wrong choices, that our species must avoid. If we would be religious, we have to sound the depths of the despair that warfare rightly inspires and find a holiness that both seconds our revulsion and shows us how even warfare does not exhaust the divine resources.

2:33: DUTY

"But if you turn away from this battle, which your duty requires, then, giving up duty and glory, you will only get trouble."

Ancient Hinduism partook of what is sometimes called "the cosmological myth." In its master-story of reality, things on earth mirrored things in heaven, and all beings shared in a single divine substance. Thus the caste system, which organized Hindu society into four principal classes (and hundreds of subclasses), claimed heavenly sanction. At the beginning, human society was formed from the sacrificial division of the primal human being (a cosmic Adam). His head became the priests, his feet became the workers, and so forth. Each of the four principal castes had its own duty. The duty of warriors, those like Arjuna who belonged to the second caste, was to administer the commonweal and defend it against unjust aggressors. "Warriors" therefore were what we would call rulers and politicians, as well as military personnel. Hindu society certainly was aware of the abuses that any of the castes could work. Priests who did not perform the sacrifices purely but rather sought only fat fees; rulers who did not administer the realm justly and wisely; merchants who were dishonest; workers who were lazy—all of these failed the Dharma and so merited punishment in a painful future life.

Nonetheless, Hindu culture feared that chaos would break out if the castes did not stick to their own duties but rather crossed lines. Better one's own duty badly done than to attempt the duty of another caste. For Arjuna to turn pacifist and oppose war—question its foundations, seek alternatives—was to threaten the stability and order of Hindu society as a whole. Thus Krishna here counsels him to fight even though it repulses him. We are not yet at the stage where individual conscience has evolved sufficiently to stand up to social pressures. The needs of the group still greatly predominate over the misgivings of the individual. Arjuna has to fight, if he wishes to retain his good name. Should he fight and win, he can expect worldly rewards: booty, power, fame. Should he fight and die, he can expect heavenly rewards: immortal glory attached to his name, recompense from the divine powers who sanction the caste duties. On the other hand, if he refuses to do his duty he can expect trouble both on earth and in heaven. Krishna therefore is appealing to Arjuna's self-interest. Even if his motives for not fighting in fact are pure as the driven snow, people will account him a coward and his future will be grim.

Is there any defense for this sort of social pressure, which of course has had its analogues in other societies through the ages? Does social duty or patriotism have a strong case when it urges young warriors to lay aside their misgivings and fight as the elders of the tribe, the rulers of the land request? No. Usually, there is not a strong defense for the position that advocates abandoning the dictates of one's conscience and doing what an outside "they" expect or request. People in the United States most recently have seen this in the case of the war in Vietnam. Whereas originally those who objected on the basis of conscience or fled the country to avoid being drafted were more condemned as cowards than praised as people of strength and insight, nowadays they are nearly vindicated. As the general public has come to the opinion that it was a rotten war, fought for bad reasons and with bad tactics, those who opposed it early now seem like prophets. The price it exacted from the bodies and souls of a whole generation, mainly men but also women, now seems far too high. It was not a just war because it was not our war and the good it sought to gain didn't balance the evils it fostered.

Still, even though the majority of wars throughout history seem similarly unjustifiable, there remains the possibility that a people will find itself assaulted by an evil aggressor and so feel forced into war. Granted that the aggressor in fact is evil and cannot be dissuaded by diplomacy or promises of strong sanctions, is it then legitimate to ask people to overcome their repugnance and undertake warfare? To put it in terms of a specific instance, were the Allies justified in going to war to oppose Hitler and Nazi Germany?

Most commentators think the Allies were justified, as we do. Hitler and Nazi Germany represented so evil a regime, with such an implacable will to rule Europe, that warfare was the only alternative to a capitulation that would have abetted the evil. The major problem that led to World War II therefore did seem like a bestial evil making for one's throat. Underneath all the impurity in the Allies' motivation and effort—all the propaganda, chauvinism, fear of losing material possessions, desire to gain money, power, or fame—the bottom line could make fighting seem a religious duty. To be for a God of justice could seem to require being against the truly Godless Nazis.

In limit cases, then, one can justify the notion of a holy war. The problem is the ease with which this justification is taken up by impure people and applied to cases where one is not limited to an either/or, a choice that truly is for or against divine justice. For many commentators, as noted, the war in Vietnam was very different from the Second World War. For many the Second World War turned impure, unjust, when the United States escalated to the use of the atomic bomb. More recently, the rationale used by United States governments to support corrupt regimes in Latin America, the Philippines, South Africa, and too many other places has come under fire as impure. It is not enough, such critics say, to brandish slogans of anti-communism. It is not enough to trumpet national security. Too often self-interest, in the crude sense of what plays into profits for American business and power for American politicians, has ousted considerations of how evil the socialist reformers really are, of what alternatives to brutal dictatorships intelligence and good will could fashion.

So the problem with Krishna's advice to Arjuna is its potential support for *realpolitik:* the view that conflict is inevitable, power is the only language people heed, and one therefore has to manage conflict so that one's own side ends up with more power. Admittedly, this judgment on Krishna's advice has the advantage of two millennia's worth of hindsight. The writers of the Gita could not know how frequently advice such as theirs, defenses of the status quo and support for people in the know who supposedly saw the big picture, would be used to justify slaughter and immense suffering. Nonetheless, it now seems clear that the detachment Krishna would have Arjuna display toward his repugnance for warfare would better have been directed against the opinion of his fellow citizens. The concern in the analysis would better have been whether the war in fact was just or necessary.

11:11–13: DIVINITY

"So the son of Pandu beheld the world with its myriad divisions standing together as one in the body of the god of gods."

Because Arjuna continued to be troubled, Krishna further expounded the traditional wisdom that supplied the foundations of Indian society. Much of this wisdom, developed in chapters 3 through 10, amounted to variations on yoga, along with descriptions of the pantheism proper to the Hindu gods. Yoga essentially means "discipline."[3] For Krishna's purposes with Arjuna, the most relevant discipline was that which quiets the senses and the mind, allowing the yogin to gain self-possession at the essence of the self. Krishna could claim that such experience justified the proposition that the self is immortal and so exempt from the punishments of war. As well, it rendered plausible the notion that divinity is the inmost reality of everything. Krishna then described his own presence throughout creation, how he passed down the ages and stretched through all places. Our text is part of Arjuna's response, when Krishna unveils the divinity and lets Arjuna glimpse its true proportions. Arjuna beholds the world unified and standing in the body of Krishna. He realizes that Krishna is prior and the world subsequent, and that the unity of Krishna bestows unity on the disparate phenomena of the world.

So appreciated, Krishna not only encompasses the world but understandably can express himself through worldly symbols. The problem then becomes which symbols to prefer when estimating what human actions are most holy, most like the ultimate reality of the godhead. In verse 11:10 the Gita describes Krishna as having many mouths and eyes, displaying marvels, being adorned with the heavens, and "with divine weapons raised as for battle." Warfare is part of Krishna's portfolio. Warfare is too important, recurring, influential a phenomenon for Hindu theology not to incorporate it within divinity. Still, the person who disciplines the self will realize the partiality of conceiving of divinity as a heavenly warrior. Such a person will not care that the gods battle, that the peoples rage. For such a person will have entered into divinity's own freedom from desires, acting without being attached to the fruits of action, doing what has to be done without fearing or enjoying it.

The peculiar tension of Hindu theology, and so of Hindu approaches to ethical problems such as peace and justice, is the presence of a power ultimate enough to explain worldly beings yet unconcerned about how such beings act. This does not mean Hindu divinity has no preferences, does not prescribe how people should behave. When Krishna professes love for those devoted to him he pledges to care for them. Implied is his desire that they thrive, avoiding evil and enjoying prosperity. Further implied is the probability that if people draw close to Krishna and imitate him, they may be able to avoid the evils of war, to enjoy the benefits of peace. But failure will not disturb the godhead.

The vision that Krishna vouchsafes Arjuna is meant to fortify Arjuna in the truths Krishna has been teaching him. One of these assuredly is the truth of caste duty: specifically, Arjuna's responsibility to fight. But another is the priority of divinity and the relative unimportance of worldly affairs, whether those be painful or pleasant. The detachment the vision could empower would allow Arjuna to move through war or ordinary social life as through a dream or a play. Unenlightened people think war and ordinary social life are real. For them, the worst life is the most painful and the best life is the most pleasant. Enlightened people have glimpsed enough of divinity and yogic wisdom to think that pains and pleasures are both relative and indifferent. The body is bound to die. The soul cannot be destroyed. War is therefore not something of ultimate moment. Nothing in the world of samsara, the realm of births and deaths, is. The only ultimate reality is the unchanging, unsuffering existence of the divinity. All else is *maya:* illusion, sport. How useful could this outlook be for advancing peace and justice?

To the Christian mind, this outlook seems to lack the seriousness of the Incarnation, and so to lack seriousness about history and personal choice. Where Hinduism has many births and deaths, and an eternal world, Christianity has only individual lives and a world that sprang from nothingness, a history that one day will end. On the one hand, therefore, Christianity has grounds for saying that choices for or against justice are momentous, even able to determine people's passage to heaven or hell (see Matthew 25). On the other hand, Christian seriousness about history could encourage people to stir might and main to prosper there, riding roughshod over all who got in their way. So Christianity developed its own sermons about detachment, trying to undercut such evils as warfare by ripping out the faulty desires on which they depended. How different was this detachment from the detachment, the not caring overmuch, one can hear in Krishna's counsel to Arjuna?

Doctrinally, the two positions were quite different, because Christianity did not accept destruction and apparent evil into the core of its notion of God. Psychologically, the two positions appear quite close, in that both became counsels to move through human affairs lightly, not clinging to anything less than God.[4] When Hindus applied such detachment to warfare, they could mount arguments either for or against fighting. War not being fully serious, one might either engage in it lightheartedly or abstain with equal lightness of heart. To be sure, the Hindu appreciation for *ahimsa* (non-injury)

31

tipped the scales in favor of abstaining. Those seeking salvation, release from the bonds of samsara, would do well to keep from hurting any living thing. The divinity pulsed in each living thing, so hurting any was attempting to hurt divinity. Ultimately, of course, one could not hurt divinity. But, one could hurt oneself in trying. Bad karma, correlated with the sufferings one had caused, would guarantee one's own future suffering.

Christian detachment similarly could be deployed either for fighting or against fighting. If the war was being promoted as just and necessary, the detachment needed was from physical life and this-worldly prospects. Thus the crusaders were promised a heavenly reward if they were to fall trying to recover the Holy Land. If the war was judged evil or ill-advised, the detachment needed was from public opinion and one's own need for peer approval.

Today dialogue among the world religions might profitably target the task of clarifying and promoting the detachments necessary for people the world over to outlaw war. These certainly would include detachment from more than one's fair share of the world's wealth and goods, detachment from more than one's fair share of influence and power, detachment from the need to dominate others and feel superior to them, and detachment from the desire for revenge. Those who have great wealth and power have to become free of them. Those who want great wealth and power have to become free of such want. Peace will not come until the majority judge it more valuable than the profits targeted in most wars. Peace will not come until people believe its coming is up to them: what they think, how they behave, what they imagine. Down the road, two potential parties to a war can find themselves so alienated that conflict becomes inevitable. At the start of a journey, no such expectation need prevail. And the journey we make with other nations in our world begins anew with each change in generations, each change in political leadership, each new wave of poets and theologians commissioned to confect new symbol systems. The myriad divisions of the world may always be reconciled in the one God, because the one God always embraces them in a divinity more comprehensive, significant, and instructive.

16:7–8: THE DEMONIC

"Demonic men do not understand either acting or turning away. In them there is no purity, or even good conduct or truth. They say the world is without reality, without foundation, without a lord, not made by one thing following another but only moved by desire."

The detached, wise personality that Krishna is trying to inculcate in Arjuna depends on divine counsel. It honors the traditions of the ancients, who thought wisdom and sanctity came from realizing how the divine moves the human heart. Opposed to such a personality is what Krishna calls demonic people. Implicitly, if not formally, they have given themselves over to powers much less than divine, powers either idolatrous (for example, money or status puffed up as ultimate goods) or hateful (alienated from true divinity). Such a demonic personality understands neither action nor detachment. It can neither do things purely nor freely abstain. Everything it thinks and does is tainted. Naturally, it projects its taint onto other people, thinking others must be as impure, as riddled by desires, as it is itself.

The root of such demonism is the denial that the world stands founded, guaranteed its meaning, by a divine Lord. Correlatively, the demonic make the will to power, the desire to possess, the key to understanding politics. In Western terms, the demonic see the world much as Thomas Hobbes and Sigmund Freud did: libido, desire, is all.

In contrast, mental health, justice, and peace alike require confessing a foundational meaning, a divine lordship, that transcends desire. They alike require moving out of the turbulent mid-zone, where wanting and striving predominate, to zones above and below that allow reality to manifest its true span. For above desire lies the rest, the peace, the non-striving of the divine, which creates effortlessly and in its own life is the perfection Hinduism describes as being, awareness, and bliss. And below desire lie the material foundations of human life—our being embodied, our being immersed in nature—that slowly but surely teach desire its unbreachable limits. Hunger, thirst, death, ignorance, aging, pain—these are but a few of the messengers of finitude, but a few of the ways our material constraints impose themselves.

But the demonic try to block out both what is above and what is below. They don't want the light that can sanitize desire, the love that can make desire creative. They don't want the solid realism of mortality, limitation. So they live in unreality, trying to deny they are connected to, formed by, both heaven and earth. They multiply needs, projects, slights, fun, to distract themselves, to avoid what is primary, always present. Primary is the silence from which we come and into which we go. Chatter, no matter how busy, how frenetic, can never completely cover this silence. Primary is the mystery of existence: why there is something rather than nothing. No mental cleverness, no glib agnosticism, can remove its lordship. The demonic are the unreal, the ersatz. To realists, their world is literally insane: mentally unhealthy, an asylum. To realists, the world communicated by modern advertising, and the world assumed by modern military strategists, often is demonic in this sense.

We can leave to another day an analysis of how advertising frequently fuels both the libidinous desire to possess things bound to give only passing satisfaction and an unreal sense of what the world as a whole most needs for its peace. Sufficient for this day is reflecting on the demonism of many military minds, as perhaps best epitomized by the policy of trying to deter the enemy from initiating nuclear war by developing assurances of mutual destruction. To date, the nuclear super-powers have made this policy of mutual assured destruction the cornerstone of their military outlook. One can hope that their moves toward mutual disarmament will lead to a repudiation of such thinking, but for that to happen a religious conversion on the order of what the Gita implies in this text would seem necessary.

What does assuring mutual destruction imply about a nation's worldview? First, that it thinks of its enemy, and perhaps also of itself, as an entity most moved by fear, the more horrible the more effective. Second, that preserving its rights, its way of life, its standard of living justifies threatening, and perhaps actually carrying out, the destruction of other people's very existence. Third, that its preservation and prosperity justify threatening, and perhaps actually carrying out, the destruction of the biosphere—rendering the earth sterile. All of this is so fantastic, in the root sense of imaginative rather than realistic, that one has to doubt the sanity, the mental balance, of the people who accept and abet it.

The counter-logic, espoused by many revolted by such a view of deterrence, is that rendering the earth sterile, bereft of life, is a sin, a freely chosen evil, so enormous that no national benefit could justify it. Similarly, destroying massive numbers of "enemy" people to preserve one's own privileges is an enormous sin and ought to be considered unthinkable. Third, that the encounter is warped from the start when people are treated as though fear were the best entree to their minds and hearts. What would be a much better way? Accepting the enormity of the bind into which the policy of mutual assured destruction, and the pessimistic view of human nature driving it, have gotten us and starting to negotiate an entirely new relationship.

In such a new relationship, the zones of transcendence and material constraint that the demonic, the libidinous, try to block out would get their due. The partners to the new negotiations would confess that they are not the measure of reality: they did not make the world, and they have no right to threaten the world's destruction. Moreover, they both have done wrong in the past and thought stupidly. They both have called non-negotiable many ideological and practical convictions that in ultimate perspective are far from absolute. We are familiar with both the Marxist and Capitalist forms of such ideological convictions. In religious perspective, both Hindu and Christian, neither is privileged or non-negotiable.

Should the state have the right to control people's lives in all details? Is it wise to attempt to straight-jacket people's minds? Is it blasphemous to try to keep people's souls ignorant of God, unfed by symbols of transcendence? No, no, and yes. Are individuals correct in thinking their freedoms take precedence over the common good? Is the capitalist state wise to leave the fate of the economy and the environment to private enterprise? Is it blasphemous to equate prosperity with material possessions and pleasure, sometimes covered with a patina of biblical language? No, no, and yes.

However gimmicky this parallelism, however much in need of refinement and nuance, it makes the point that the superpowers, and the other nations who hew to their Marxist or Capitalist lines, are similarly if not equally demonic. In both sorts of regimes the mid-world of desire dominates. In both transcendence and realistic material constraints, God above and nature below, get short shrift. The result is that in both the citizenry are pressured toward mental illness, amnesia, ignorance of the most basic realities. No wonder both populations put up with a diseased military policy. No wonder both countenance leaders who live in a dream world, who seem unable to comprehend the proportions of what they would have their nations be prepared to do.

Lately ethicists have popularized the question, May a nation in good conscience threaten what it may never morally do? The answer clearly is no. If it is wrong for me to murder you, it is wrong—unreal, immoral—for me to bully you by threatening murder. If it is wrong to deploy noxious chemicals in warfare, it is wrong to threaten such deployment, to possess such weapons, to negotiate as though one would manufacture them if one's desires were not granted. All the more so with nuclear weapons. Any people who believe the world has reality, is well-founded, and has a Lord should be able to follow such logic. If they cannot, Krishna would question what their professed beliefs in fact mean.

18:64: LOVE

"Listen again to my highest word, the most secret of all. You are loved by me surely, and I will tell you for your good."

Bhakti, the religious pathway of love, uses this text as a great warrant for human beings' approaching divinity with the confidence of people well-loved. In contrast to the austere, impersonal divinity of the Upanishads (the philosophical texts at the end of the Vedas), the personalized deity we find in the Krishna of the Gita shows human beings warmth and care. This is the highest word, because it imparts the most longed-for revelation. It is the most secret word, because prior ages of Hindu culture had not known it, had not dared think it. How could puny, bent human beings solicit the divine love? What were men and women, creatures of a day, to the divinity that had always been and always would be? Why should what was full being, awareness, and bliss concern itself with what was pitted by desire, enslaved to the cycle of death and rebirth? Only because of the goodness of divinity itself. Hinduism, like Christianity, finally makes God the cause of what God does. Nothing outside of God forces or tempts the divinity into action. If divinity loves needy humanity, or decides to take a physical form in human beings' midst, that is entirely divinity's own doing.

Still, it is good for human beings to know this about God. It is good for us to contemplate being the apple of God's eye, dear to the divinity. For then we may have the self-confidence, the ego-strength, to deal with other people patiently, even lovingly. Then it may strike us that if God has so loved us, we ought to love one another—forbear one another's wrongdoings, beat our swords into plowshares.

Psychologically, it is clear that much human aggression and animosity spring from fear and a lack of confidence. People who don't think themselves strong, don't feel comfortable, don't like themselves are more apt to commit criminal acts than people who are at home with what they have hitherto become. And while the best predictor of psychological health is the home life people had as children, even those who got off to a bad start can be healed, recast, by feeling the divine love. That is why contemplation is one of the most important tools for establishing justice and peace.

In contemplation, whether Eastern or Western, people try to deal with ultimate reality holistically, heart-to-heart. Meditation implies disciplining the mind. Contemplation implies activating the heart, sending one's love out to the divine mystery, letting the divine mystery show its prior presence in the depths of one's being. Regularly, contemplatives report experiencing the no-thing-ness of the divine. Regularly, they become engaged with a blank, cloud-like whole that defeats their best efforts to reason or will their way to clarity about it. In fact contemplation can seem like the death of the meditative, ratiocinative mind, of the dogged, virtue-mongering will. It forces the whole personality to allow itself to be reset in something opaquely yet undeniably prior, deeper, higher, vaster—the length, height, breadth, and depth of divinity itself.

Listen to how Ma Jnanananda of Madras, a contemporary Hindu guru, describes her experiences of *samadhi,* the goal of yogic contemplation: "She said that she had experienced this deep absorption many times since she was a child. She added that when one is finally fixed in it, there is no more ego. Now that absorption is always the background of her consciousness. *Samadhi* is an experience without content and yet is not empty. It is complete fullness. 'In that state I used to ask myself, "Where am I?" Then I would try to think of myself at some point, but immediately I felt myself to be at the opposite point. In short, it is a feeling of being simultaneously everywhere. But there is no perception of the physical world. The physical world is dissolved in the unity.' "[5]

A Western contemplative, Christian, Jewish, or Muslim, no doubt would describe deep experience at prayer somewhat differently. The Indian tendency to dissolve the world in the unity of the Ultimate makes Indian mysticism somewhat acosmic. But Western contemplatives report that the love of God takes them outside themselves and shows them the unity of all things. They report what the theologians sometimes call "panentheism": God is in everything (without being contained by anything), and everything rests in God. Moreover, East and West, contemplation heals people of their ills, their sins, their fears, their despairs. It tells them in direct, irrefutable ways that their world has a meaning, a solid foundation, a loving Lord. If Jesus was transported from death to resurrection by the mere inreach of the Father, we have a dramatic case of what contemplation says the Spirit does regularly for lesser people. Regularly, the Spirit (divinity given and received) takes people apart from the cramped, distorted horizons that have been twisting their minds and souls. Regularly, the Spirit insinuates the love that all people crave, crooning like a mother in the night that all will be well. If the Spirit, the divinity come into our minds, hearts, souls, and strengths as love, in fact is embracing us, all has to be well. What more can human beings ask than to be united with God, the deathless, the all-good? What less can satisfy the immense, insatiable yearning of the human spirit at its best? And what resource is better able to secure people in the mature sense of self-worth necessary for peace-making?

In the strategies that target mutual assured destruction, we discerned a pessimistic view of human nature and an option for moving people by fear. In the economic strategies that speak of the survival of the fittest and construe the world as a jungle where the strongest deserve the best spoils, one can discern a similar pessimism. Human beings being bent, savage, self-serving, sinful creatures, the best that governments can achieve is tying them round with laws, lashing them with penal or social sanctions. Because most political scientists, theoretical or practical, know nothing more intimate to human beings than libidinous energy to dominate, flee pain, and pursue pleasure, they are powerless to indicate such sources of healing, renewal, and creative overtures toward peace as the love of Krishna, the joy of the Holy Spirit.

This remains true despite the stunning example of the best peace-makers, present as well as paradigmatically past. Jesus and the Buddha are perhaps the premier examples, West and East, of people so contemplative, so divinized, that peace waved out from them like an eighth day of creation. Gandhi and Martin Luther King, Jr. galvanized the past generation of idealists. More recently, such Nobel Peace Laureates as Desmond Tutu and Elie Wiesel have updated the classical blend of contemplation and realism, faith and politically effective love. The fact that these *mahatmas,* these great souls, are dismissed by professional politicians and soldiers as idealists (if not cranks) shows the depths of the conversions peace now requires. The well-educated American of recent years, even more than the average person in the street, has so little understanding of contemplation, so little intellectual grasp of the world opened out by the divine mystery, that he or she is bound to dismiss it as unrealistic, irrelevant to the great secular tasks of making peace in the global village and creating more just institutions in every land.[6]

For the contemplative, by contrast, only grasping the true dimensions of the world, only knowing what Krishna and Jesus have intimated, gives us either the vision or the creativity to make progress toward peace and justice. People generally cannot do more than they can conceive, and they cannot conceive more than what they are. So they have to be refashioned, reformed, taken beyond what workaday, let alone cynical, human judgment considers natural to something "supernatural," something that frees human beings to be and do their best. That something is the love promised by Krishna, lived out by Jesus, felt at least fleetingly in all our peak experiences. Because such love seems fleeting and fragile, we have to look on work for peace and justice the way we would look on a marathon: as something very demanding, yet in fact possible if we can get ourselves in shape. Because when we experience such love it becomes credible that we have been embraced by the creative force that made the universe, looking on work for peace and justice can bring us to sing, spontaneously and surely, "We shall overcome some day."

Discussion Questions

1. What is the healthy reaction the prospect of warfare and killing should arouse?

2. How should we come to grips with the record of humanity's thousands of wars?

3. What sort of duty has a state to protect its citizens?

4. What sort of duty have soldiers, politicians, and ordinary citizens to avoid warfare?

5. What difference does it make to envision the world, with all its diversity, as subsisting within divinity?

6. What aspects of divinity are expressed in warfare, the destructions of natural evolution, the explosions of the stars, and the naturalness of death?

7. How does libido relate to the demonic?

8. How does a healthy, adequate view of reality's span contextualize human striving and start to heal it?

9. What are the practical implications of Krishna's, divinity's, finding human beings dear, beloved?

10. Why is contemplation useful, perhaps essential, to peace-making?

Notes

1. For all the traditions we treat, the best comprehensive reference work is *The Encyclopedia of Religion,* 16 vols., ed. Mircea Eliade (New York: Macmillan, 1987), hereafter cited as ER. On Hinduism see Alf Hiltebeitel, "Hinduism," ER, vol. 6, pp. 336–360. Good general introductions include A.L. Basham, *The Wonder That Was India* (New York: Grove Press, 1959); Thomas J. Hopkins, *The Hindu Religious Tradition* (Encinco, Calif.: Dickenson, 1971); David R. Kinsley, *Hinduism* (Englewood Cliffs, N.J.: Prentice-Hall, 1982); Troy Wilson Organ, *Hinduism* (Woodbury, N.Y.: Barron's, 1974).

2. All of the verses from the Bhagavad-Gita are adapted from the translation by Ann Stanford, *The Bhagavad Gita: A New Verse Translation* (New York: Seabury, 1970).

3. See Mircea Eliade, *Yoga: Immortality and Freedom* (Princeton, N.J.: Princeton University Press/Bollingen), 1970.

4. For a profound meditation on detachment and graceful action, see Anonymous, *Meditations on the Tarot* (Amity, N.Y.: Amity House, 1985), pp. 3–26.

5. Charles S.J. White, "Mother Guru: Jnanananda of Madras, India," in *Unspoken Worlds: Women's Religious Lives in Non-Western Cultures,* ed. Nancy A. Falk and Rita M. Gross (San Francisco: Harper & Row, 1980), p. 27.

6. One does not have to accept all of Allan Bloom's de-

scription in *The Closing of the American Mind* (New York: Simon and Schuster, 1987) to agree that recent American education has lost much of the wisdom enshrined in both the perennial philosophy and the documents of the American founders.

Chapter 3

BUDDHISM AND THE DHAMMAPADA

THE BUDDHIST WORLDVIEW

As an Indian religion arising around 500 B.C.E., Buddhism assumed many of the concepts we elaborated when discussing the Hindu worldview. Gautama (ca. 536–476), who became the Buddha by achieving enlightenment, agreed with the Hindu holymen who had been his teachers that desire was what kept people in the prison of *samsara*. After trying various austerities, he opted for a middle way that disciplined the body but kept it healthy (able to support the spirit in its quest for liberation). The Buddha articulated his experience of enlightenment in what have become known as the "Four Noble Truths": All life is suffering; the cause of suffering is desire; to remove suffering one must remove desire; the way to remove desire is to follow the noble eightfold path of right views, right intention, right speech, right action, right livelihood, right effort, right mindfulness, and right concentration. The first two paths pertain to wisdom: a proper understanding of reality. The middle three paths pertain to morality: fitting action. The final three paths pertain to meditation: getting one's mind in shape. Wisdom, morality, and meditation therefore have functioned as the tripod on which Buddhist practice has rested.

Buddhism, like Hinduism, thinks in terms of karma and rebirth. It tends to speak of ultimate release as *nirvana*, rather than *moksha*, but the differences between the two terms are slight. Where Buddhism does alter its Hindu heritage significantly is in its concept of self or substance. Hinduism tends to equate the *atman* or self with the *Brahman* that is the foun-

44

dational reality of the cosmos. Atman and Brahman, the Upanishads (and the Vedanta philosophy based on them) say, are one. For Buddhism there is no self, no permanent substance underlying all the accidents or properties of either people or sub-human beings. Rather, all existents are self-less, painful, and fleeting. Reality is a coordinated dance with nothing in, under, or behind the dancers. What you see or experience is what there is. No Brahman hides within, giving an ultimate meaning. As some Buddhist philosophers later put it, nirvana and samsara (ultimacy and karma-conditioned existence) are one. Alternately, one might say that all beings are "empty." None has an "own-being" that stands outside change, fleetingness.

Some Buddhist thinkers discoursed on these ideas rather academically, but in the main these were not items for armchair analysis. In the work of the Buddha himself, and throughout the mainstream of the Buddhist tradition, they were pastoral, therapeutic tools. Thus the Buddha was reluctant to debate the metaphysical implications of the Four Noble Truths, to discourse on nirvana, to get sidetracked into discussions that did not "edify": bring people closer to realizing liberation. Traditions such as Zen virtually did away with philosophizing, insisting that meditation was the be all and end all of Buddhist living. To be sure, Zen Buddhists depended on the great branch of Buddhist thought known as the Mahayana and were convinced that meditation had a dialectical relationship with action. But they distrusted ideas and talky analyses. It was more important to experience enlightenment than to know its definition.

Regarding peace and justice, the Buddhist tendency has been to think that if people were enlightened, or even well schooled in the Dharma (Buddhism, like Hinduism, uses this term for "Teaching"), the sort of behavior considered desirable would occur rather effortlessly. Still, Buddhism did elaborate five ethical precepts binding on all believers: Not to kill, not to lie, not to steal, not to commit unchaste acts, and not to take intoxicants. These five precepts of *sila* (custom, ethics) have bound both laity and monks as a minimal behavioral code. What they, like the Four Noble Truths, meant in concrete circumstances depended on further elaboration.

Walpola Rahula, who has written a very helpful digest of Buddhist views entitled *What the Buddha Taught,* describes the Buddha's views of war and peace as follows: "It is too well known to be repeated here that Buddhism advocates and preaches non-violence and peace as its universal message, and does not approve of any kind of violence or destruction of life. According to Buddhism there is nothing that can be called a 'just war'—which is only a false term coined and put into circulation to justify and excuse hatred, cruelty, violence and massacre. Who decides what is just or unjust? The mighty and victorious are 'just', and the weak and defeated are 'unjust'/ Our war is always 'just', and your war is always 'unjust'. Buddhism does not accept this position.

"The Buddha not only taught non-violence and peace, but he even went to the field of battle itself and intervened personally, and prevented war, as in the case of the dispute between the Sakyas and the Koliyas, who were prepared to fight over the question of the waters of the Rohini. And his words once prevented King Ajatasattu from attacking the kingdom of the Vajjis."[1]

In this context, we should note that Buddhism, like Hinduism, has taught the desirability of non-injury (*ahimsa*). One should deal with all creatures as gently as possible. Thus certain occupations (butchering, soldiering) were proscribed as incompatible with the Dharma and vegetarianism was the ideal. Moreover, perhaps the paramount Buddhist virtue has been compassion. Buddhists were to look upon all living things as suffering from ignorance, entrapped in the meshes of the cycle of death and rebirth, and so deserving compassion. What became known as the Bodhisattva vow was a formal commitment to postpone one's own achievement of nirvana so as to labor for the salvation of all unenlightened beings. The Bodhisattvas (saints, Buddhas-to-be) were not just models of Buddhist holiness but also effective forces for the liberation of those who came under their sway. In East Asia the most popular Boddhisatva was Kuan-yin, who functioned much like a Mother Goddess, offering refuge to the suffering and sinful.

Because of its acceptance of the doctrine of karma, Buddhism has sometimes seemed slow to promote what the West calls social progress or social justice. In principle Buddhism rejected the caste structure of Indian society, and also the male chauvinism that made Hindu women fit for moksha only when they had been reborn as men. In practice monks outranked laity in prestige and women did not have equal access to authority within the Buddhist community (*Sangha*). Nonetheless, Buddhist monasteries often provided such socially helpful works as schooling and medical treatment, along with care for wayfarers and poor people, while Buddhism as a whole usually acted as a brake on warfare and cruelties toward the vulnerable.

The Buddha himself, and Boddihisattvas who stood as models of Buddhist perfection, largely fitted the profile of the yogic saint. They were detached, composed, full of peace. Their compassion for suffering humanity showed in their efforts to teach people a better way, an enlightenment that would take them beyond the reach of most suffering. But they recognized that people finally had to accept such instruction, take it to heart, and expend personal effort. If given individuals or groups did not take the Dharma to heart, that probably was due to their bad karma. The job of the preacher was to offer them the word, the chance to glimpse the light. The job of the saint was to model compassion and peace. Beyond that, what happened lay on people's own heads. Still, the Buddha could be eloquent and forceful in urging people to own up to their painful condition and seek the remedy of the Dharma, as his famous Fire Sermon shows: "Bhikkus [monks], all is burning. And what is the all that is burning? Bhikkus, the eye is burning . . . with the fire of lust, with the fire of hate, with the fire of delusion; I say it is burning with birth, aging and death, with sorrows, with lamentations, with pains, with griefs, with despairs."[2] One might therefore call the Buddha a fireman, bent on watering desire down. In other contexts, the imagery is therapeutic: healing diseased spirits. But always the accent is practical and the tone is urgent—as urgent as a being full of peace, light, detachment, and contentment can make it.

9/121: EVIL

"Let no man think lightly of evil, saying in his heart,
It will not come nigh unto me. Even by the falling of
water-drops a water-pot is filled; the fool becomes
full of evil, even if he gathers it little by little."[3]

For a succinct orientation to the Dhammapada (*The Path of the Teaching*) one is not likely to do better than Geoffrey Parrinder's lines in his useful work *A Dictionary of Non-Christian Religions:* "[The Dhammapada is] the most famous scripture of the Buddhist canon. It is a short work of 423 verses in twenty-six chapters. It teaches moral and mental discipline, includes the Four Noble Truths and the Noble Eightfold Path, and teaches taking refuge in the Buddha, the Law [Dharma] and the Order [Sangha]. It says that a man [person] should 'overcome anger by non-anger, let him overcome evil by good'. A version in the Gandhari language was discovered near Khotan in central Asia in 1892, written on birch bark, and dated to the first or second century A.D., thus being the oldest surviving Indian religious text. *The Dhammapada* comes towards the end of the *Sutta Pitaka,* the second major division of the Buddhist canonical scriptures. It is so short that many Buddhists know much of it by heart."[4]

We are dealing, then, with a beloved portion of Buddhist tradition. On the whole, the Dhammapada is more moralistic than meditative or philosophical (concerned with wisdom), but of course it assumes Buddhist philosophical convictions and seriousness about meditation. The very first verse of the work supplies its guiding conviction: "All that we are is the result of what we have thought; it is founded on our thoughts, it is made up of our thoughts. If a man speaks or acts with an evil thought, pain follows him, as the wheel follows the foot of the ox that draws the wagon."[5] All important to the Dhammapada, therefore, is how people think, what thoughts (images, symbols, goals, desires) fill their spirits.

In the text we are focusing upon here, "evil" tends to occur in a personality not anchored in the goodness the Dharma would inculcate. From such an unanchored personality come the outer acts—of murder, lying, stealing, fornication, and drunkenness—proscribed by the five basic precepts of *sila*. From many people floating free of Buddhist virtue come the wars, cruelties, injustices, and sufferings that plague societies in every age and every place. So the Dhammapada would make people mindful of how evil approaches, how not being stabilized in Buddhist virtue and truth can slowly move people to wrongdoing.

First, one should not take evil lightly, thinking that because to date one's virtue has stood firm one is beyond temptation, could never be corrupted. The implication is that evil can insinuate itself into any heart. People need only stop being vigilant, stop making progress along the path of virtue, for evil to slip up on them. Second, most evil-doing comes from people who were corrupted little by little. The image of water dripping into a pot is an artful touch. We take little notice of such small increments, and yet before we know it the pot is full. Third, for Buddhism evil-doing and foolishness are two sides of the same coin. Buddhism does not speak of sin. It is not absorbed with the mystery of iniquity that tortures biblical thought. If one is enlightened, one will not do evil. If one does evil, one is not enlightened. Evil-doing is foolishness pure and simple because inexorably, inevitably, it binds the evil-doer to the wheel of karma and so to more suffering. Justice, in the Buddhist scheme of things, above all is the intrinsic law that as one thinks and does, so will one become. Do wrong and you will be wronged—by yourself, if not by others. Do right, live well, and your substance (the collection of "heaps" of impressions that makes up your selfless identity) will flourish, perhaps also your material fortunes. Unlike the Deuteronomic theology of the Hebrew Bible, the Dhammapada does not assure us that doing well will bring material prosperity. However, it does assure us that doing well will bring better karma and so progress toward nirvana.

Verse 122, following on our text, is its positive image: do not think lightly of good, thinking it will not come, because good can fill a man bit by bit, like drops of water filling a water pot. In both verses, the ending phrase is significant: "even if he gathers it little by little." Day by day, act by act, we add to our evil or good. The Dhammapada does not take up the problem of our human mixedness—how we are both evil and good, whether adding evil pushes out goodness and adding goodness pushes out evil. It is fairly simplistic in its psychology and exhortation, but often the more profound for that. Here, as in many other places, what it wants to drive home is both obvious and subject to human amnesia: we make the personalities we end up with. Whether we advert to it or not, we are becoming worse or better, stronger in evil-doing or stronger in doing good.

If we take peace-making and advancing social justice as species of doing good, we can apply the insights of the Dhammapada to how individuals are likely to experience their contributions. Becoming peace-makers, and so children of the New Testament God, is a matter of a dialectical interplay between what we do and what we are. Like most of the other virtues, being peaceful and just are expressions of one's core goodness. This does not mean one doesn't have to join specific efforts, doesn't have to make choices about where to apply one's political leverage. But it does mean that working for peace and developing peaceful attitudes is not something one adds on to such other spiritual tasks as praying, loving God, being responsible on the job, being good to one's children, or participating in the sacraments. Anything that opens the heart to God and people in need, that fills the mind with holy wisdom and aspiration, makes one a peace-maker and agent of justice. For any such thing stabilizes one in the primacy of the divine love, which in turn makes the idiocy and repugnance of human hatred, disorder, and strife all the clearer.

The contrary is that people who start closing their hearts to God and other people in one area, on one matter, set up a process primed to spread to other areas. Racists are easily sexists. Religious bigots easily think that bombing the infidel would please God. What we think and do have consequences. The Dhammapada is most interested in the psychological consequences: how they shape an individual's character.

Today we should be at least as interested in the structural consequences: how attitudes become popular, held by many, institutionalized, made the rationales directing our activities in business, government administration, military preparations, religious education. People thrive or suffer from such structural consequences. Poor people more easily find help or rejection. People concerned with the spiritual life—education, the arts, scientific research, prayer—find the going easier or harder depending on how popular consciousness has come to regard those activities. Funding, personnel, equipment, time—all the ingredients of a venture, a project, now tend to be subject to institutional reviews that beg their philosophy, their sense of the bottom line, from the popular consciousness without. How good or bad, how wise or foolish, the people offering such a philosophy or interpreting it are has much to say about what other people will experience in hospitals, unemployment offices, welfare offices, army training camps, junior high schools, research foundations. The peace a society has it in mind to target and the peace a society actually achieves stem largely, though not wholly, from the peace in its citizens' hearts. The same with a society's justice. Each day, little by little, individuals are adding drops of peacefulness or belligerence, of indifference or concern, to a great water-pot.

17/223: ANGER

"Let a man overcome anger by mildness, let him overcome evil by good; let him overcome the niggard by liberality, the liar by truth!"

Chapter 17 deals with one of the principal roots of evil-doing: anger. Bodily anger, an angry tongue, and an angry mind all offer the Dhammapada object lessons in what the virtuous Buddhist has to bring under discipline. Positively, a person who is not "sunk in self" and is detached will avoid anger and sufferings. The implication is that much anger, and the evil-doing it prompts, expresses self-centeredness and attachment. Often, although not always, we are angry and lash out because we have uncontrolled desires—for material gain, or applause, or the sweet taste of success. Since Buddhism aims at removing suffering by removing desire, it has to think of anger as a sign of disorder, of desire not yet routed.

Before taking up our stated verse, we may also note that this chapter shows signs of being well aware of the provocations to anger anyone of us is sure to suffer. Consider, for example, the matter of criticism. As the text puts it (v. 227), whether we keep silent, speak much, or use only a few words, there is sure to be someone to blame us. Everyone in the world comes in for criticism. It is not just a national pastime, it seems coextensive with the human species. If the Buddha, Jesus, Gandhi, King, Mother Teresa, and other paragons of virtue have been fiercely criticized, even martyred, we should not be surprised to find ourselves sliced up by sharp tongues.

In our text, the outlook is more positive. Mildness can overcome anger. Good can overcome evil. Generosity can

overcome stinginess. Truth can overcome lies. Such an outlook has some empirical data to warrant its hopefulness, but
probably it depends more on an act of faith. Believing that
mildness, goodness, generosity, and truth are congenial to the
human being, things that make it grow and feel right, the
Dhammapada is convinced that such virtues will prove more
powerful than their contraries. No doubt the Buddha and the
Buddhist saints gave flesh to this conviction. No doubt the
treasury of Buddhist teaching stories had many tales of how
simple monks or nuns had converted people who initially
hated them or sought their harm. But the deepest reason for
the Dhammapada's confidence probably was the authors' own
sense that genuine virtue is attractive, appealing, something
that calls those who observe it to go and do likewise.

Admittedly, virtue also can provoke hatred. People mired
in vice can see the good as accusations and so wish them to
go away, even to perish. But mildness can overcome anger, as
the saying about honey catching more flies than vinegar suggests. Goodness can overcome evil, because the soul finds evil
ugly, dirtying. Liberality shows magnanimity, a breadth of
soul, an openness of heart, that shames niggardliness. Lies dis-
tort the spirit of the liar, twisting the mind and heart, as well
as polluting social life, whereas truth pleases the mind and
heart, seems what the spirit is made for, and enriches the fund
of social trust.

If all this is so, overcoming the anger ingredient in much
war-making amounts to showing the angry a more excellent
way. Often the angry will claim they are seeking justice or
vengeance. Sometimes they will claim that anger is the proper
response to evil. Sometimes they will be right. As Robert
McAfee Brown has noted, recalling Saint Augustine, hope has
two beautiful daughters, anger and courage.[6] Often, however,
the anger that gets us into strife contributes to a spiral of
charge and counter-charge, hurt and retaliatory hurt. Unless
something breaks the spiral, violence and suffering are likely
to escalate. Usually that something is a spirit, a person, who

can think and feel beyond retribution. Usually peace-making demands renouncing memories of past hurts, however bitter, and proposing mutual forgiveness.

Another implication of the Dhammapada's attack on anger is the importance of the means we use when we try to improve situations. Modern political thought has questioned the precept that the end does not justify the means. Thus governments now routinely engage in covert operations, knowing that were they to be frank about their espionage, sabotage, and even murder they would certainly risk, and probably suffer, an onslaught of outrage. It is the discovery of their actions, the publicizing of their immoralities, that daunts them. Were they assured of secrecy, many of them would suffer few qualms. Thus the French showed no more signs of genuinely repenting of their sabotage of the ship protesting their nuclear testing in the Southern seas than the Americans showed over linking covert operations with Iran and the Nicaraguan Contras. In both cases the embarrassment was that they had been caught in something stupid, something that made a lie of their public professions. In neither case did covert action itself, or the sabotage of innocents, come up for serious review, let alone for condemnation.

To the mind of the Buddhist, you cannot produce good fruit from a bad tree—a species of the doctrine of karma compatible with New Testament convictions.[7] You will not get good effects from actions bad in themselves or in the intention behind them. Only peaceful people will make peace. Only just people will generate justice. And if we may criticize much Buddhist ethics for seeming to neglect the influence of social factors—structural, institutional, legal, and other matters—we should not miss the significance of this analysis of what must be present in the agents of peace and justice.

Being grounded in meditation, and believing in the significance of spiritual forces, Buddhists, and other traditional religionists, often were able to appreciate the holistic, subtle, more than pragmatic aspects of human encounters better than we moderns. Yet even we know that whether people like one another influences how well they are able to do business together or adjudicate legal differences. Similarly, we know that when encounters shrink to the purely legal or bureaucratic they are bound to leave at least one of the parties feeling dehumanized. Again and again commentators on negotiations for arms reduction, peace, land reform, labor contracts, and all sorts of other settlements underscore the importance of building mutual trust. But what makes for mutual trust more than telling the truth? What is more destructive of negotiations, relationships, efforts to achieve harmonious collaboration than lying? The same with mildness and anger, generosity and stinginess, goodness and evil. One must embody the goodness of the new relationship one is trying to achieve. One must greatly control, ideally remove, the bitterness one has felt if the divorce proceeding is not to reopen, perhaps worsen, old wounds.

Buddhist compassion, allied with Buddhist detachment, has much to teach us about purifying our motives, breaking the cycles of recrimination, and generating proposals that truly seek just settlements rather than new advantages. Politicians of course have a great responsibility to create honest, credible dealings among the nations. But so do the press and the general populace. If parties to a negotiation feel they have to emerge victorious, to be perceived as having gained more than they sacrificed, they will be bound to think of one another as adversaries. The press and the general populace should help them think of one another as partners, collaborators. So many of our problems now are international, common to many nations, that thinking in terms of partnership, or simply in terms of common victimhood, is well warranted. Environmental pollution, threat from nuclear arms, terrorism, maintaining a stable world economy, and a dozen other issues involve us all, even when some of us have been oppressors and others oppressed. Buddhism, thinking that all life is suffering, can minimize the distinction between oppressors and oppressed. Urging detachment and the voiding of anger, it can maximize the chances for fruitful negotiations. So although the Dhammapada is two thousand years old, much of its advice remains startlingly relevant. We can never dismiss the significance of the mentality people bring to their negotiations. Detachment and compassion will always be in great demand.

19/256–257: THE JUST

"A man is not just if he carries a matter by violence; no, he who distinguishes both right and wrong, who is learned and leads others, not by violence but justly and righteously, and who is guarded by the Law [Dharma] and intelligent, he is called just."

True to its psychological interests, the Dhammapada approaches the matter of justice by focusing on the just personality. And the first ingredient it finds required is non-violence. People can win, prevail, predominate, but if they do so by violence what they achieve is unjust. It cannot contribute to the long-range common good, because the means it has employed themselves increase the common evil. Violence, in the Buddhist scheme of things, virtually always carries the implication of increasing bad karma. No matter what its outcome, it will snare those who employ it more tightly to samsara.

For a full ethical discussion of this matter, we of course would have to gain more precision about "violence" and question whether in certain circumstances it isn't justified to oppose destructive force with a destructive counterforce. As we saw in the quotation from Walpola Rahula, however, Buddhism has little sympathy for the doctrine of just warfare. On its reading of history and human nature, claims to be using violence to redress injustices or defend the innocent usually are bogus. Whether one actually can live in the political world and prosper through non-violence of course has been much debated. The people who saw the success of Mahatma Gandhi as a concrete proof that non-violence could accomplish great social change heard the response that Gandhi was fortunate to be dealing with the British instead of with the Nazis. Even when one has reminded the respondents that Indian and Irish victims of British massacres don't consider themselves fortunate, the question remains: how does one deal with foes, aggressors bent on one's destruction, when they seem deaf to reason, so obsessed with ideological justifications for their aggressions (which they tend to call retaliations) that they think their cause holy, an imperative of conscience or history. In recent years Marxist and Islamic ideologues have posed this problem all too bloodily.

The Buddhist response tends to be that one will only gain the conviction that violence virtually always is counterproductive if one can transcend this-worldly, secular or temporal perspectives. The Buddhist ethicist is interested in the long haul: what happens to the community of living, suffering beings as a whole? Will a given action bring them closer to freedom from samsara or will it further burden them with bad karma and so more suffering? Compared to the millennial rhythms of the struggle to escape samsara, particular conflicts can seem quite transitory. Thus Buddhist monks were willing to die, if need be by suicide, to protest the violence of the Vietnam war. Thus Gandhi prepared his *satyagrahis* (followers committed to using only the force of truth) to suffer the assaults of British troops without striking back, and if need be to die for the cause of Indian liberation.[8] The case for Christian pacifism is not so plain, but on its side is the example of Jesus, who suffered injury of all sorts without resorting to physical violence (Jesus did give his opponents many a tongue-lashing). At the least, then, the person aspiring to be considered just, one who builds up fairness and prepares the ground for peace, must seriously consider embracing non-violent means. At the least, the insights of Hindus such as Gandhi, of Buddhists such as Gautama, and of Christians (or Jews) such as Jesus ought to give one long pause before joining violent retaliations, let alone violent initiatives.

Perhaps this is also the place to consider the integrity of the individual agent and turn over the proposition that workers should not be expected to assume stances, casts of mind, that disturb their own religious peace. To put this concretely, one can ask whether a Gandhi, a Gautama, a Jesus wasn't constrained, even determined by non-violence because violence so jarred with his relation to God or ultimate reality? Could anything have persuaded Gandhi to pick up a rifle or throw a bomb, or was he so convinced of the purity of Truth and the impurity of most human motivation that it was virtually impossible for him to imagine a situation justifying such an action? Could anything bring Mother Teresa to bomb the government buildings in Calcutta as a protest against the political foundations of the poverty that brings people into her hospice to die before their natural time? When one is religious to the point that God or Buddhanature is the foremost reality in one's life, does assaulting other creatures for the sake of temporal improvements become unthinkable? Or, as some liberation theologians argue, does the injustice, the cruelty, the torture that grinds people down year after year, condemning the majority in many lands to wretchedness, represent an evil so great that in the name of religion—adherence to God—opposition to such injustice becomes a moral necessity (and sometimes justifies a violent response)?

This is a very difficult question, all the more so when it is posed by Westerners who do not accept the doctrines of karma and samsara. One can solve part of the problem it poses by agreeing that opposition to injustice and the causes of suffering is requisite for all who want to be considered children of a living, caring God. The dispute then can shift focus and concentrate on the legitimacy of violent means of expressing one's opposition. More precisely, the dispute can focus on whether non-violent means are efficacious enough to warrant restricting just, holy opposition to non-violent methods. And then, with such a focus, one may be able to clarify such matters as patience and impatience, injustices so regular they call for both moral conversion and political revolution and injustices that seem abuses of a system better will and intelligence could salvage.

Our own sense is that Buddhism, and to a lesser extent Christianity, counsels a strong prejudice in favor of non-violent means, but that one cannot rule out the possibility that in extraordinary circumstances it may be necessary to use force, violence, to avert the continuance of massive evils. Such circumstances would raise the possibility of arguing that violence can be the lesser of two evils. Dietrich Bonhoeffer, the Protestant theologian who lost his life for opposing the Nazis, reasoned this way when he approved efforts to assassinate Hitler.

Of course, such an argument easily becomes a slippery slope leading to justifying assassinations, covert sabotage, and a host of other violent actions that now are regular features of our political landscape. Let a group find its situation an enormous evil, an intolerable injustice, and by the doctrine of choosing the lesser of two evils it can try to justify constant violence, even terrorism. From Ireland to the Middle East, one sees that sliding down this slippery slope is not merely a theoretical possibility. In the tactics of a Lenin, it became business as usual.

Once again, then, the ethics of peace and justice shows itself to be much more than simply sketching out a few precepts. People have to judge, in their quite concrete circumstances, how they may legitimately combat the evils twisting their own lives, the lives of those they love, and the lives of their brothers and sisters around the globe. The anger at such evils that is necessary if we are to remove them must not escalate into something blanket, something that takes over our souls. Working for peace, being a religious revolutionary, tests one's ethical maturity as few other ventures. Probably we feel the sharpest influence of religious convictions at the point where we agree that there are some measures we will not take, some responses we rule out of court. Probably being religious means having a God or an ultimate reality always greater than human affairs, even the most pressing. By this criterion, neither the atheistic (materialist, feminist, other secular) totalitarian nor the totalitarian who urges holy war in the name of God can be considered a worker for true peace, one walking the path that is straight and truly helpful. By this criterion, all who make their earthly cause more basic or important than the divine mystery are a potential menace. (Also ripe for criticism, however, are those whose religious or secular convictions inculcate no passion to work for peace and justice—those whose well-springs do not become incarnate as practical love of neighbor.)

24/357: HATRED

"The fields are damaged by weeds, mankind is damaged by hatred; therefore a gift bestowed on those who do not hate brings great reward."

Here the proposition is that hatred is to humankind as weeds are to a field. In neighboring verses (356, 358, 359) the same figure is used for lust, delusion, and craving. Each is like weeds, destroying the fertile field of human endeavor, the rich harvest human nature might yield. Thus any gift that rewards, encourages, nurtures the contrary (freedom from lust, hatred, delusion, craving) brings a great reward. Presumably, the reward is twofold: the benefactor is blessed, improved in karmic condition, for having forwarded the Dharma and humanity's happiness, while the recipient of the gift, stabilized in virtue, becomes an abettor of human welfare at large. In the second case, humanity itself is rewarded.

Once again, the Dhammapada is working with convictions, assumptions, somewhat different from those that have predominated in Western ethics. Buddhist philosophy thinks of dispositions and actions as deploying a quite physical causality. A vice such as lust or hate is a physical force bound to find an outlet and make an impact. One may call it a character defect, but the character it malforms is embodied, an agent in the physical world. And the physical world itself is an ecosystem, an overlapping, interacting series of niches that living beings inhabit. Any vice has an impact on this karmic field, makes a ripple in the well of the total human reality.

How do weeds damage a field? Without claiming agricultural expertise, we can propose the commonsensical view that they choke more beneficial growths—grass, wheat, vegetables. They make something that to the human observer is rank, unproductive, an eyesore. Of course the figure verges on anthropomorphism but as a spontaneous moral image it seems quite clear and unobjectionable. Vices prevent the growth, the beauty, the sustenance society needs for its moral health. Vices keep people from advancing toward nirvana, from achieving peace, from rendering one another justice, from making a prosperous common life.

The implication of such a figure, when found in a moralistic treatise such as the Dhammapada, is that one should tear out the vice. As the way to improve the field is to weed it, so the way to improve the human situation is to "vice it": strip it of what is noxious, ideally by ripping out the root. Of course Buddhism does not think only moralistically. Its meditational and wisdom interests keep it from collapsing into a behavioristic, probably puritanical effort to root out all vice. Wisdom and meditation supply the vision, the calm, the detachment, in which the virtues can flourish. The virtues—strengths of character, good (enjoyable) habits that more prescind from vice than struggle constantly with vice—flourish best when they are pursued not for their own sake but as the logical, natural, even easy consequence of a great vision, experience, love. Thus the Buddha, having gained enlightenment, did not have to work much at particular virtues such as freedom from lust (chastity) or freedom from hate (benevolence). His personal field had been cleaned and fertilized by the light that had flooded him. Equally, he did not have to target vices for demolition the way a housing authority marks the map for the wrecking crew. Most vices had little appeal. Most temptations were so gross, so ugly, they were unthinkable. The same with the sort of love that pulsed in Jesus' heart. Orthodoxy has always taught that Jesus was fully human but without sin. In addition to the important corollary that sin is nothing essential to humanity (human nature), this teaching suggests that Jesus had much better things to do and love. He was free to go where his work, his Father, his love of people and desire to improve their lot took him. No untoward, disordered love of money, sex, power, or other worldly goods deflected him.

When we turn these thoughts toward peace and justice, we find variations on several by now familiar themes. First, there is the theme that disordered love, wrong passion, unjustifiable desire is at the root of most great evils such as war and rampaging injustice. Second, there is theme that evil is not reasonable or natural but rather constitutes a mystery: something whose existence we cannot comprehend. Divinity, too, constitutes a mystery, something we cannot comprehend, but significantly differently. In the case of divinity, or what Buddhists might call ultimate reality (Buddhanature, nirvana), the problem is such intelligibility—goodness, reasonableness, beauty—that it exceeds our capacity. Divinity and Buddhanature are not conditioned, finite, delimited as we human beings, or any other creatures, are. So there is a mismatch between what they are and what we can comprehend. Their mystery is by way of surplus or plentitude. The mystery of evil is by way of mindlessness. Evil is a surd, something we cannot understand because it is not understandable. It is somewhat like trying to cut a diamond with a candle: it doesn't fit, work, compute. So in one sense evil is not real: we cannot perform the acts of imagination, insight, and judgment we normally must go through to verify that something does in fact exist. We have to approach evil by way of negation or privation: an order that ought to obtain does not. A proportion, harmony, reasonableness we rightly expect we cannot find. Peace, the classical Western definition of which is "the tranquillity of order," has been replaced by war, which entails the disorder of people battling over goods furnished them all by mother earth, of people trying to destroy life none of them created. Justice, which connotes balance, fairness, each party receiving its due, has been replaced by its lack: an injustice that tilts the scales, brings it about that many starve while a few throw out good food as garbage, that many are homeless while a few have dozens of empty rooms. That sort of imbalance makes no more sense than war. We may trace its history, studying how the given economy got to the point where housing didn't match up very well with people to be housed. We may illumine the psychology of marketing, purchasing, feeling entitled, feeling left out, not being able to manage a budget, not being fit for most jobs. But we can't get our heads around the central distortion, the core irrationality. It is something that should not, that need not be.

And yet it is, and it is more noxious than the figure of the weeds in the field can convey. Because war, injustice, racism, sexism, murder, physical abuse, and the other species of sin, evil, and vice clearly are noxious, most people accept that they should not be, accredit the pain in their hearts and the cry on their lips that protest. On the other hand, by no means all people, perhaps only a minority of people, think they need not be. "Things were ever thus" is true enough to tempt us to make war, injustice, and other great evils natural to humankind. Buddhism, Christianity, the other religions, and some humanisms have done great work, been perhaps most salvific, by denying that evil has to be. True, the denial has been nuanced: evil is likely to be strong, but evil is not something concomitant with human nature, not an expression of what our species is, like being embodied, having speech, making art. Therefore we can limit evil. Therefore we can discover more humanity by weeding our souls and body politic. In the beginning we may find this hard work, but as it progresses—as the field clears and better crops replace the weeds—it becomes congenial. The person who rewards freedom from hatred therefore is a great benefactor. His or her gift promotes fuller humanity, than which there is nothing greater (except the divine and angelic modes of being).

26/390: NOBILITY OF SPIRIT

"It advantages a Brahman not a little if he holds his mind back from the allurements of life; in direct measure as the wish to injure declines, suffering is quieted."

The brahman lived in the highest caste of Indian society and so could symbolize the noblest human achievements. Although brahmans had as their specific work performing the Vedic sacrifices and instructing people in holy lore, both men and women born into the brahmanic caste enjoyed respect and high status simply by that fact. Once again, the doctrine of karma supplies the explanation. The popular understanding of caste joined it with one's merits from previous lives. If one was a worker, located in the lowest caste (we prescind from discussing the untouchables, whom all four castes were supposed to avoid), one had to think that one's karma had determined this ranking. Insofar as Hinduism generally taught that people were more likely to reach moksha from the brahman caste than any other (although this was not ironclad), it favored brahmans as those closest to salvation and so purest and wisest.

The Dhammapada takes over this ancient Indian prejudice and reworks it so that "brahman" becomes synonymous with "noble," "having a well-developed humanity." Part of the reworking stems from the fact that Gautama, the Buddhist paradigm of enlightenment and development, came from the warrior caste. Another part stems from Buddhism's criticism of both the caste structure of Indian society and the sacrificial religion ("Brahmanism") prevalent at Gautama's time. The caste structure seemed to ignore the main point—inner achievement, actual enlightenment—in favor of so extrinsic a factor as birth and consequent social position. The sacrificial religion, too, seemed extrinsic, almost a magical effort to control the world by sacred sounds, and to the mind of the Buddha it was impotent to liberate most people.

So in our text the "brahman" is the true Buddhist, the person become rich in humanity, noble in achievement, a model of the wisdom that brings nirvana. The whole of chapter 26 is concerned with describing features of such a person, but our verse is less expectable, more creative than many. For, first, it stresses that the thing to hold back from the allurements of life is the mind, implying that lust, warfare, economic manipulation, and the other vices begin with wrong thinking, badly directed desire (not a new thought, but one quite radical in its implications). And, second, it focuses such restraint on the wish to injure, to harm, to give pain (most likely in response to pain given). Above all, we might say, the good Buddhist, the noble person, keeps the mind from wanting to punish other people—whatever their provocation. Third, and most intriguingly, the Dhammapada opines that in the measure the wish to injure declines, suffering is quieted. On the one hand, this is obvious: if fewer people wish other people injury, there will be less attacking, hurting, warmaking, and violence in the world. This, in turn, will mean less suffering. On the other hand, the psychological bent of the Dhammapada makes it likely that such objective, socially obvious suffering is not the text's real interest. More in keeping with the general bent of the Dhammapada is an interest in the suffering of the subject who is misguided or possessed. The Dhammapada probably has in mind monks and pious laity who are likely to meditate on its teachings. They have little need to be reminded that the will to hurt causes much misery in the world and that diminishing the will to hurt will diminish the quota of objective suffering. But it may have escaped them that when people give up their desire to hurt, thin out their bile, they themselves suffer less. That is the connection, the equation, the Dhammapada likely is dangling before the reader's eye.

How does the will to injure cause suffering in those who possess it, indulge it, excite it? By immersing them in samsara and karma. By roiling their souls and taking away their peace. By setting them up for frustration, if they are not able to execute their wish and hurt their enemies, or setting them up for the backlash of such enemies. To our mind, the text is deepest where it approximates the insight of Thomas Aquinas that sin injures the sinner, making the sinner one bound to suffer. Insofar as wanting to hurt others, imagining with pleasure their pain, plotting how to make them pay for the wrongs they have done, and similar mental preoccupations work on a person's soul, they bring disorder and so pain. Like a bone pushed out of joint, they are bound to make the whole organism twinge. Insofar as such thoughts actually proceed into action, they involve the body in their disorder and so reenforce it, give it the added reality of having been uttered by the tongue, prosecuted by the hand, tasted as adrenalin and bile. Such bodily experiences make our will to hurt weighty like a potent symbol. What previously had only been imagined now has been tried. The difference is the chasm underscored by liberation theologians. The soldier who has been in battle is quite different from the soldier who has only been in the classroom or on the parade ground. The surgeon who has only studied the anatomical charts is quite different from the surgeon who has done the procedure a hundred times. So too with the patient, the victim. To have been operated upon is far different from having contemplated the procedure and recovery. To have oneself been shot, or knifed, or tortured is far different from what others were able to communicate to one's intellect.

The Dhammpada does not deal very much with this zone of praxis. It is satisfied with contemplating the stimuli of actions, the thoughts that make people want to do hurt. Certainly they are less lethal than the actions that carry out the hurting, but in some ways they are less realistic and so harder to correct. When we act on things—in fact go to war, drop an atom bomb, savage an enemy village—an unforgiving, ineluctable reality confronts us and demands acknowledgment. The ashes, cinders, maimed bodies stand as our accusers, forcing us to realize how horrible "war" actually is. For months our nerves and dreams won't let go of what we have done. What we have done therefore lodges in us, becomes part of us, stays as near as horrible memory. Thereby, it makes it hard for us to contemplate repeating such actions in the future. We now know the cost of acting on our violent desires and usually it seems too high.

In contrast, the cost of thinking about injuring, brooding on our hurts, imagining sweet revenge more easily escapes us. The cost is a personality not knowing the things for its peace. The cost is the foolishness of placing part of one's happiness at the mercy of a history tangled, wrong, from the start. The wrong done to us has started the story of our relations with so-and-so off on the wrong path. If we respond, we go further along that wrong path. If we stew in our juices, we let the wrong permeate our whole soul. The only way to heal ourselves, to right the story, is to move to a new path. There the way forward is to forget the wrongs done, let go of the past pain, maybe even forgive our enemies their stupidities and twistedness. Even though popular culture tells us we have been had, others have put something over on us, in our better moments we know those who have tormented us are worse people. It feels shameful to have been a victim. We may continue to call ourselves naive or weak. But we can let go of that, too. If we can get our minds in good shape, we can let the whole mess fall away, like the dirty clothes one drops before entering the shower. Under the stream of Buddhist peace, we can let it all sluice down the drain. All that we are comes from what we have thought. If we think pure thoughts, happiness will replace our misery, as surely as the wheel follows the ox.

Discussion Questions

1. Why do Buddhists say there is no self?
2. How do wisdom, meditation, and morality figure in the Four Noble Truths?
3. Why does the Dhammapada lay so much stress on our thoughts?
4. How does desire relate to evil-doing?
5. What sort of anger is a daughter of hope?
6. How does egolessness diminish anger?
7. Can non-violence embolden evildoers?
8. How much of the Buddhist ethic of non-violence is acceptable if one does not believe in karma?
9. What are the ways in which desire gives life energy and spice?
10. Would it be good Buddhist doctrine to desire peace?
11. How attractive do you find the portrait of the brahman?
12. Why would it be especially important for brahmans to develop compassion?

Notes

1. Walpola Rahula, *What the Buddha Taught,* 2nd ed. (New York: Grove Press, 1974), p. 84. For general background on Buddhism, and further bibliography, see Frank E.

Reynolds, Charles Hallisey, *et al.,* "Buddhism," ER, vol. 2 (New York: Macmillan, 1987), pp. 334–439; Richard H. Robinson and Willard L. Johnson, *The Buddhist Religion* (Encino, Calif.: Dickenson, 1977); Tevor Ling, *The Buddha* (London: Temple Smith, 1973); Edward Conze, *Buddhist Scriptures* (Baltimore: Penguin, 1959); Edward J. Thomas, *The History of Buddhist Thought* (New York: Barnes & Noble, 1951); Edward Conze, *Buddhism: Its Essence and Development* (New York: Harper Torchbooks, 1959); *Buddhism: A Modern Perspective,* ed. Charles S. Prebish (University Park: Pennsylvania State University Press, 1975); and Antony Fernando, *Buddhism Made Plain: An Introduction for Christians and Jews,* rev. ed. (Maryknoll, N.Y.: Orbis, 1985).

2. Rahula, *What the Buddha Taught,* p. 95.

3. The translations from the Dhammapada are all from *The Dhammapada,* trans. Irving Babbitt (New York: New Directions, 1965).

4. Geoffrey Parrinder, *A Dictionary of Non-Christian Religions* (Philadelphia: Westminster, 1971), p. 77.

5. Babbitt, *The Dhammapada,* p. 3.

6. See Robert McAfee Brown, *Religion and Violence,* 2nd ed. (Philadelphia: Westminster, 1987), p. xxii.

7. See Roger Corless, "New Testament Passages Apparently Consonant with the Buddhist Notion of Karma," *Buddhist-Christian Studies* 6 (1986), 141–144.

8. See Erik H. Erikson, *Gandhi's Truth* (New York: W.W. Norton, 1969).

Chapter 4

CONFUCIANISM AND THE ANALECTS

THE CONFUCIAN WORLDVIEW

Prior to the Communist takeover in 1949, for more than two thousand years China had been under the spell of Master Kung—Confucius (551–479 B.C.E.). Although Buddhism and Taoism had their periods of predominance, Confucianism made the greater contribution to expressing and forming the native Chinese worldview. In his own mind, Confucius was not an innovator. He was passing down and applying the example, the ideas, the convictions of the great sages of yore. Because the days in which Confucius lived saw considerable strife, the Master was convinced that the wisdom of the ancients was desperately needed. Because he could not get an emperor, or even a territorial lord, to appoint him chief political counselor, the Master was gloomy about the prospects for political improvement. Deprived of the official influence he coveted, the best he could contribute was tutoring to youth who might be influential in the years ahead: young men (the Master did not teach women) of talent or influential family.

The main lesson that the wise leaders of yore exemplified and recent generations had forgotten was the primacy of moral virtue. Instead of trying to rule the people and achieve prosperity by force, the worthy ancients led by good example. Confucius was convinced that such example could again lead the people to the paths of prosperity, and disciples such as Mencius stressed it even more. For while Confucius thought that virtue and learning were relatively rare accomplishments, Mencius thought that they so befit human nature, so expressed what humanity was primed to become, that they were relatively easy: seeing them well-modeled would do half the job.

For Confucius, the two great virtues that learning was to develop and maturation entailed were goodness (*jen*) and ritualistic propriety (*li*). The one was more interior and the other more exterior. Goodness (humaneness, love) involved what Buddhists might call right intention, right action, and right feeling. Confucius thought that he had only gained it, and so consonance with the Way of the ancients, when he reached seventy. At that point, his long years of striving to improve his character yielded full fruit and he could do what he wished, because what he wished completely coincided with the Way. He had no desires that were not directed to virtue. His only longing was to be full of humaneness: wisdom, helpfulness, peace.

Li bore on the delicate social interactions that Chinese culture had long entailed. One had to know how to deal with people of different stations properly and gracefully. One had to know how to perform or attend the many different rites that marked the different seasons of the agricultural year, occasions of state, and moments of transition (birth, marriage, death) in family life. Especially significant was the time of a parent's death, because filial piety, complete devotion to one's parents, was the cornerstone of Confucian social order. Ideally, children would withdraw from social life for a lengthy period (as much as three to five years) to mourn the passing of the one who had given them life and formed their character.

Herbert Fingarette has probed the significance of *li* with a sensitivity to what we moderns miss by having removed it from high rank among our list of virtues.[1] When interactions follow protocols that all know and observe, they more easily achieve both grace and force. Because people do what is expected, what custom has shown brings good results, they are bonded to one another as people short on ritual seldom can be. We might say that such attention to outer forms helps to fashion inward character: people slowly become what they regularly do. To be sure, ritual carries the danger of formalism: independent personality becoming lost among the letters. The Confucians did not avoid the charge, and the reality, of being stuffy, perhaps even hypocritical. On the other hand, their influence helped China remain a unified cultural zone for tens of centuries, and their influence continues beneath the surface of Communist China today.

In Confucius' day, the rituals of social life presupposed the cycles of nature. The Way of the ancient sages reposed in the Way by which the cosmos moved. Lao Tzu, author of the *Tao Te Ching,* stressed this cosmological dimension more than Master Kung, but Confucian thought (indeed, virtually all pre-modern thought, East and West) fully accepted it. To be in harmony with nature was to place oneself in the way of prosperity. To be out of phase with nature, running against the cosmic grain, was to court disaster. China never clarified the divine aspect of the natural world as clearly as truly polytheistic cultures did, but from spirits attending water holes and ghosts keeping strong the influence of the dead to a generalized sense that rulers only succeeded when they enjoyed the mandate of Heaven, traditional, Confucian China gave the Way of nature and the ancients a theophanous (godbearing) glow.

In the Confucian scheme of things, therefore, the hierarchical relationships that promoted social prosperity were fitted into the patterns of nature. They were, one might say, an expression of natural law—not merely a matter of human contriving or convention, but something embedded in "the way things are." These hierarchical relationships included the subordination of children to their parents, of wives to their husbands, of subjects to their rulers, and of younger siblings to their older brothers and sisters. In addition, China thought hierarchically about such main social rankings as emperors, court officials, regional administrators, soldiers, merchants, and peasants. These rankings did not have the clarity or force of Indian castes, but peasants expected to obey gentry and governmental officials were honored personnel. Indeed, when Confucian thought became the basis of the civil service examinations that governmental personnel had to pass to obtain office, it ensured that this hierarchical thinking would be the official public philosophy. (Taoist and Buddhist thought on the whole functioned more privately, for the nourishment of personal development and art.)

Confucianism usually is presented as a humanistic philosophy, and it is true that the Master thought caring for politics, in the broad sense of human well-being, was more than enough work for tutors and rulers to carry out well. On the other hand, the Master accepted the influence of the spiritual, supernatural domain and famously said that those who neglected heaven left themselves with no ultimate recourse (3:13). We sometimes forget that in traditional societies there was no "humanism" in the sense of an outlook that has rejected the supernatural or transcendent dimension. In China, as in India, the continuum of existence continued on from inanimate-plant-animal-human to spirits-gods-Heaven (ultimate principle). Taoists, Buddhists, and Neo-Confucians frequently exposed their spirits to these latter realms through meditational exercises. The substratum of ancient belief that preceded Confucian rationalism gave a large place to shamans, diviners, exorcists, and others who interacted with the spiritual, occult world. To this day astrology and geomancy have an important role in Chinese culture. All of this provides context for Confucius' stress on reason and moral cultivation.

On the one hand, it suggests that Confucius could assume that people knew about, accepted, and factored in the spiritual force of spirits, ghosts, Heaven, local deities, and the like. On the other hand, it suggests that Confucius thought the way forward, the thing most needed, was more rational control and fuller moral cultivation. People without a good hold on the principles of the ancients easily could become superstitious and fatalistic. People without solid training in the virtues, without effective character formation, would probably be captive to their passions. Effective rule, and effective citizenship, demanded more self-possession than Confucius saw the going education and political thought of his day providing. Until people knew the classics, in both letter and spirit, they were not likely to cooperate toward a social regime in which *jen* and *li* prevailed.

3:13: HEAVEN

"Wang-sun Chia said, ' "Better to be obsequious to the kitchen stove than to the south-west corner of the house." What does that mean?' The Master said, 'The saying has got it wrong. When you have offended against Heaven, there is nowhere you can turn to in your prayers.' "[2]

The *Analects* are not a work Confucius composed. Rather, they are more like an anthology of his sayings. And while the anthology as a whole seems a credible indication of the Master's point of view, scholars debate how authentic individual sayings are. In most cases, we will never know whether Confucius himself actually uttered a given saying, or whether it was composed by a disciple as the sort of saying the Master was wont to utter. It is much like the situation with the sayings of Jesus. Like the historical Jesus, the historical Confucius probably is beyond recovery. On the other hand, the Confucius who shaped so much of subsequent Chinese culture, like the Jesus who shaped so much of European culture, was the master who spoke from the pages of the canonical text. Whether he had in fact uttered a given saying became less important than the impact that saying had through the centuries. In the case of Confucius, tradition finally attributed to him not only the Analects but such other works of the Confucian canon as *The Great Learning.* Some even thought he had composed *The Book of Changes* (*I Ching*). Still, the Analects has remained the work considered closest to the historical Master in both teaching style and actual words.

Our text here is the one referred to in the previous section. Note the literary form of the saying: a disciple is asking the Master to clarify a point from tradition. This form is reminiscent of the *responsa* used by teachers of Jewish law, and it has analogues in most other religious traditions. Thus we have Sufi questions and answers, incidents where the disciples question Jesus and are enlightened, dialogues between the Buddha and his followers, examinations of and by Hindu gurus. They remind us that traditional religious education was something living, oral, and holistic. Students generally lived with their teacher, absorbing not just what the teacher thought, or how the teacher interpreted tradition, but also how the teacher lived. The teacher was as much a model as an oracle. The education was more an apprenticeship or a novitiate than a series of lectures and seminars.

As such, the education assumed the common sense, the popular culture and tradition, of its time. In this saying, we get a glimpse of the family piety of the typical Chinese family. The south-west corner of the house was the place of honor. All directions had their significance, some being auspicious and others inauspicious. Such a sensitivity to directions and natural forces, which one finds in other ancient peoples like the American Indians, bespeaks a closeness to nature, an immersion in the cosmological myth (the master-story that makes the cosmos a single organism), that modernity has left behind. The kitchen stove obviously is a symbol, but of what the commentators debate. A main-stream interpretation takes it as an epitome of this-worldly concerns: warmth, food, joy in the household. Like the hearth, it could stand for the good life of domestic prosperity and happiness. Perhaps it even had overtones of mammon. So the saying that Wang-sun Chia wants the Master to elucidate probably had a significance something like, "One should pay more attention to practical affairs than to reverencing hallowed places or forces." As such, it seems a set-up for Confucian humanism. Wang-sung Chia would be giving the Master a fastball right down the middle, expecting him to knock it out of the ballpark and crush those who clung to old, superstitious ways.

The Master does no such thing. With considerable authority, he rejects the traditional saying. How well-regarded the saying was we do not know, but something in the attitude of Confucius suggests the mentality of Jesus when he imposed a similar authority: It was said to you of old, an eye for an eye and a tooth for a tooth. But I say to you, love your enemies, and do good to those who persecute you (see Matthew 5:21–38). The true Master does not hesitate to correct tradition, even when he reveres it and wants to save each jot and tittle. He is confident that his inner grasp of the tradition, his inspired wisdom, tells him what the tradition in fact ought to be saying in a given situation.

When you have offended against heaven (when you have neglected the south-west corner of the house, the place of the shrines), there is nowhere for you to turn in your prayers. The presumption here is that you must pray. Perhaps the prayer is only the cry that comes from the heart when suffering strikes. Perhaps it is only the rush of gratitude that begs release when a new child is born or an old child is saved from possible injury. But pray you will, Confucius suggests, because to pray— reach out to the mystery holding your world, petition the Source and the End—is human. If you don't have such thoughts, emotions, desires, you are dead to the mystery, the puzzle, the nest of concerns that most define your species. So Heaven, the realm of the ultimate powers, the home of the mystery, is as intimate to you as you are to yourself. It enters into your definition, what you are as a human being, as fully as blood, bones, and nerves. Cut yourself off from heaven (an ontological impossibility, but for many a psychological fact) and you will have no recourse—nothing less capricious than human fate, the contest of human animals, to which to take your cause.

How much of human prayer, what percentage, has flown to heaven over the years in pursuit of a peace that would overcome domestic or national strife, of a justice that would stop the hurting, the unfairness, the pain that need not and ought not to be? Of course not even the best of bookies could give you the actual odds, but every likelihood is that a great deal of people's religion through the millennia has sought peace and justice. To say this is not to dismiss or diminish purer worship, which praises divinity for its own sake. It is not to forget the sacramental tales most groups have told themselves to keep refashioning their identity. It is simply to reassert the tie between religion and human need, between worship and human pain. Divinity could of course reveal itself simply for the splendor of it. The Buddha might have had a splendid career teaching people about the joys of an enlightenment that wasn't concerned with therapy. But in fact the gurus, the masters, most people have followed have offered a wisdom that was saving, healing, reconstructing. Thus Confucius did not content himself with offering an abstract, detached political science. His goal was teaching that reformed people's hearts and so might refashion their social lives. At a time when strife was spreading blood and tears everywhere, he spoke of traditions, points of view, that might turn things around.

In our interpretation, therefore, this text represents a Confucian conviction about the primacy of one's relationship with Heaven. Get that relationship straight and you will have cleared the deck of the idols that spur most wars, that create most injustices. Confucius, like such modern philosophers as Henri Bergson and Eric Voegelin, was interested in an open soul. He wanted the roof of the psyche to roll back, or at least have a skylight, so that divinity might shed the light and warmth necessary for solid health. The brute fact is that without such light human beings grope in a darkness that makes butchery and great pain all but inevitable. Without a reverence for the divine, creative mystery that relativizes all the wealth, power, territorial possession, fear, vengeance, and other great motives for war and injustice, war and injustice are sitting on the doorstep, perhaps even lifting the knocker. For Confucius, as for Plato, the state is the individual psyche writ large. Have disordered people, ministers of state and commoners alike, and you will have disordered nations, disordered history. Set the people in order under Heaven, help them open their souls, and you will have laid open the bedrock, the taproots, of human prosperity.

3:26: DEFICIENCIES

"The Master said, 'What can I find worthy of note in a man who is lacking in tolerance when in high position, in reverence when performing the rites and in sorrow when in mourning?' "

It should be clear by now that the Eastern religious classics have a prejudice about how to attain social order—peace and justice. They think social order depends on ordered people—rulers first of all, but the average person as well. We shall see that the Western religious classics are little different. The Gita, the Dhammapada, the Analects—all stem from a time when political science was concrete, little different from ethics. All, in fact, stem from a time when philosophers were aglow with the discovery that the individual personality need not be at the mercy of the crowd, is more than a member of a herd. True, they did not live in individualistic societies where rights were more significant than duties. The common weal still was more important than private pleasure or happiness. But they were close to the discovery of the ties between public and private order. They were still aflame with the realization that one could only prescribe what would make for justice and peace if one knew them from within, as virtues ruling one's own soul.

Much of the drama of the Platonic dialogues comes from this realization. Throughout Buddhist history it has been a great spur to spreading the practice of meditation. Christians have thought similarly in urging conversion and prayer. In each case, the guiding insight, tacit or express, has been that individual agents finally are responsible for the myriad acts that make up a public order or disorder. Even when one focuses on decisions, orders, that change history by enlisting thousands of others as their executors—decisions to go to war, to change previously racist practices, to allow abortions, to introduce the vernacular into the liturgy—someone finally has to take responsibility, has to give an accounting in terms of how an order in his or her own soul sought replication in the body social. Moreover, each execution of this history-shaping order from on high came from an individual person, whose personal order or disorder entered in. For the masters of religious wisdom, there are no human actions exempt from the law that what is done expresses what people are at the time they do it. The good news stemming from this is that the world is not a moral chaos, a great machine no one is running. The bad news is that all the agents who have disordered souls, who are ignorant of the import of their actions, amount to a great roadblock to progress, create a massive collusion with evil-doing. To choose is to forward social order or hinder it. Not to choose is to do the same. Even to obey, to do unthinkingly or thinkingly what others command, is to agree that what has been commanded ought to go forward and contribute to the incarnation of the order or disorder behind it.

In the present text, Confucius rather bitingly dismisses people who lack what he considered essential virtues. They were not "gentlemen," people of breeding and good character who were contributing to good social order. Indeed, they were part of the problem, contributors to the disorder Confucius was dedicated to removing. First, there is the person in high position, the ruler or leader or overseer, who is intolerant. By rejecting him, Confucius implies that those who are on top, handling great responsibilities, have to be flexible and understanding. They ought to have the experience to know that people all have their idiosyncrasies. They ought to have the perspective, the grasp of the whole, to realize that there are many ways of realizing one's overall goals. If they cannot adapt their strategies to fit the actual conditions of the people they encounter, they are bound to botch the job. Indeed, they may make good policies turn out to have disastrous effects. One can see this happening again and again in both national governments and church groups.

Interestingly enough, what most promotes tolerance at the top is a profound grasp of essentials. People who have plumbed the human condition and know their tradition to its bedrock are able to shift smoothly and adapt as circumstances require. It is like teachers who truly understand their subject-matter. They can illumine it with a dozen different examples, thereby making it clear to students at various stages of development. They are the polar opposites of ideologues, as are good rulers. When one understands, or knows clearly what one wants to accomplish, tolerance and flexibility flow quite easily. Confucius had mastered his own trade. He knew in his bones the good order exemplified by the ancients of yore and the great classics. So he had little respect for people in authority who had not similarly mastered their trade. They were amateurs and bunglers—a great burden to all forced to work under them.

Similarly, what could he say about a person who lacked reverence when performing the rites? Once again, only that such a person didn't know what should have been known and so was a social menace. In Confucius' day, the rites were a form of social cement. Through them people acted out the convictions on which Chinese political order depended. Therefore to carry them out irreverently was to attack the foundations of social order. It was to pry loose the building blocks and invite the forces of chaos to wave in. Irreverence in fact was an offense against Heaven, which finally sanctioned the rites. It was a person's more or less knowing revolt and atheism. Because these were not private matters but matters of civil, public religion, they could not be left to people's individual whim. They were too closely connected to the inward peace that led to outer peace, to the inward justice that led to outer justice, for the Master to consider them innocuous. One can see that things have greatly changed since Confucius' day. With the rise of cultural pluralism and the predominance of individual rights over common responsibilities, Confucius' despising of irreverent people is bound to seem strange, even bigoted. Why was it any of his business? Because he knew that common rites are the expression of a common mind, and that a common mind is the basis of the friendship, the neighborliness, necessary for a prosperous community.

The third defect that gives the Master offense is people's not sorrowing when mourning. Here the need to connect *jen* and *li* is perhaps clearest. If one does not feel sorrow when mourning a parent or a friend, what has the mourning ritual become? A modern mentality has great difficulty with this question, because a modern mentality is well aware that emotions are not at the beck and call of reason. Further, it thinks honesty, authenticity, is more important than outward displays. Confucius was well aware of such problems, but he would not accept them as a license either to avoid prescribed rituals such as mourning or to carry them out hypocritically, merely for form's sake. No, his high ideal was to match inner disposition with outer action, and he gave low marks to people who couldn't achieve this, especially in so capital a matter as mourning the passing of one's parents.

Death should always be an occasion for mourning, even when it comes to strangers or people whose sufferings make it a relief. For death makes human existence tragic—burdened by a pain that sears into the human soul. If we do not have the humanity to recognize this and find it in each instance of mortality, from the infant stillborn to the nonagenarian passing quietly in the night, we have considerable maturation still to achieve. If we do not find in the need for mourning at death a powerful motive for avoiding war and bloodshed, we are part of the problem peacemakers have to solve. This is partly a matter of imagination and partly a matter of will. One has to recognize the pathos of human existence, as that culminates in death, and so be led to go gently with all human flesh. One has to resolve to lessen such pathos, or postpone it, as much as one can, letting the intimations of resurrection and immortality contribute their encouragement. Here, in this statement from Master Kung, we find a reminder of the negative form of the golden rule: Do not do unto others what you would not have them do unto you. Do not fail to mourn when others die or suffer, as you would not want them to fail to mourn for you. Do not be blind, obtuse, unfeeling about others' pain, as you would not want them to ignore yours. Such failures of imagination and will, such inability to mourn, understand, and sympathize, explains huge amounts of strife and injustice in our world. If more teachers followed Confucius in despising them, without failing to sympathize with the people they rule and ruin, we would have more eloquent and effective assaults on the causes of our world's so great pain.

4:5: BENEVOLENCE

"The Master said, 'Wealth and high station are what men desire but unless I got them in the right way I would not remain in them. Poverty and low station are what men dislike, but even if I did not get them in the right way I would not try to escape from them. If the gentleman forsakes benevolence, in what way can he make a name for himself? The gentleman never deserts benevolence, not even for as long as it takes to eat a meal. If he hurries and stumbles one may be sure that it is in benevolence that he does so.' "

The topic here is *jen.* The Master's main point is that nothing is more precious to the true gentleman, the full human being, than such inner goodness. With benevolence, people can endure many hardships. Without benevolence, outer success is merely a charade.

Note, first, that Confucius is shrewd about what motivates most people. Wealth and high station are prominent in virtually everyone's ideal life. China was not a land in which poverty and humility were paramount virtues. Buddhism introduced monastic poverty and preached egolessness, but Buddhism came on the scene half a millennium after the Master had made his mark. No, the native tradition that Confucius expressed and shaped thought of the good life in terms of longevity, wealth, and high station. To be comfortable, honored, and surrounded by numerous great-grandchildren was to have gained the Chinese acme. On the whole, the Chinese did not expect immortality (Buddhists, and some Taoists, were the exceptions, but in their cases one has to qualify what "immortality" meant). So to place benevolence above wealth and high station was to challenge the Chinese mainstream.

For Confucius, getting wealth and high station by improper means—either by crime or by compromising one's integrity—vitiated their attainment. He could not think of enjoying them at the price of sacrificing benevolence, which meant that he could only think of enjoying them if he had gained them honestly. The Master would have been quite content to have been employed by a ruler as chief political advisor, compensated handsomely, and given high station in the land. That fit quite well with his life's ambitions. Similarly, he was quite content to receive the accolades of his pupils and bask in their esteem. Such things were only fitting. But here he shows that his sense of his own worth did not need outer acknowledgments or rewards. The first person he had to please was himself. Enjoying a good conscience, the experience of being rightly ordered, was far more important to him than enjoying money or fame. So the criterion of what success he would accept and approve became what success squared with his conscience, harmonized with his benevolence.

That meant that, were he to fall into poverty and low station through no fault of his own, he would not worry. Despite what popular opinion in his day (as in our day) tended to think, there was nothing shameful about poverty and low station. People of integrity, benevolence, brought low their by circumstances are no less gentlemanly, humane, than they would be had circumstances, fortune, been kinder. So Confucius would not try to escape a poverty he had not brought on himself by his own folly or inhumanity. Indeed, throughout most of his life he had to live frugally, traveling from state to state in search of a patron and teaching such students as his reputation brought him.

Many discussions of social justice rightly involve judgments about poverty. Generally, people who would reform going arrangements so as to make the economic and political orders more just target poverty as the enemy. And, on the whole, they are correct. Poverty grinds people down in spirit as well as body. It tends to sap their willpower, just as it makes their children hungry. A well-ordered society would share its wealth so that all people had the essentials necessary for a decent life: sufficient food, clothing, housing, education, medical care. Moreover, it would make these basic needs of the many more important than the luxurious wants of the few. Benevolence, flourishing humanity, is hard put to think otherwise. If I have a superfluity of goods and you lack necessities, how can I fail to make over to you what I don't need without failing in benevolence, *jen?* If the goods of the earth are for all the earth's people, as Western religious instinct has held, then no one has the right to luxuries while someone else lacks essentials. First things first. Only when the basic needs of all have been met should a society license people to pursue and enjoy goods that merely amuse, adorn, entertain. Saying this should not mean supporting a puritanical view of creation, of course, nor should it mean denying that leisure is the basis of higher culture: art, science, religious contemplation. However, saying it should mean supporting the view that people are more equal under the heaven that makes its rain to fall, its sun to shine, on just and unjust alike than they are unequal.

So, poverty that springs from a failure to appreciate the basic equality of human beings and their organic relatedness rightly is considered an enemy of peace and justice. On the other hand, the poverty that comes because one will not compromise one's core vocation to benevolence, or because one is more interested in the goods of the soul than material goods, can be the outward expression and effect of inward freedom. Thus the poor but noble scholar has been a venerable figure in both Confucianism and Judaism. The monk wed to poverty has been a model of holiness among both Buddhists and Christians. Those poor in spirit are blessed because the Kingdom of Heaven is concerned with spiritual treasures: love, understanding, community. Those free to go where benevolence takes them, free to succor the needs of the suffering at home or abroad, often wear their poverty like a badge of heavenly blessing. In the spiritual life, "poverty" and "wealth," like "life" and "death," can easily become tantalizing, paradoxical terms.

Thus the Confucian gentleman never deserts benevolence, not even when doing so could gain him a much-wanted meal. His benevolence is himself. Confucius seldom focused on women, and the culture of his day assumed they were less significant than men. But in our day everything said about benevolence as the crux of humanity clearly applies to women as fully as men. If they stumble hurrying to do good deeds, or to attain what their children need, one should count it no fall from benevolence. If they bear their poverty, their being on

welfare, their suffering prejudice without losing their benevolence, we should count them high achievers. Of course they
long for wealth and high station, for their families as much as
themselves. But if they know that wealth and high station do
not guarantee benevolence, their not having wealth and high
station will detract little from what they accomplish. Religion
ought to help people believe this. When it does not, when it
joins the ranks who bow to wealth and high station, it joins
the fighters against God. Confucius was no monk, but in de-
limiting the significance of wealth and high station he joined
the many monks and nuns who have reminded the world that
full humanity, and so full success, take people to a realm
where their salaries and public reputations are quite secondary compared to the love in their hearts.

4:25: VIRTUE

"The Master said, 'Virtue never stands alone. It is
bound to have neighbours.' "

The love in people's hearts makes them attractive to others. Because they are benevolent, people wishing and doing
others well, they are perceived to be friends. The same with
the other virtues. Insofar as they manifestly benefit the common good, they make those who possess them attractive. Thus
magnanimity, honesty, fairness, compassion, and all the other
good qualities, fine strengths of soul, in which moral philosophers such as Confucius have traded are attractive: powers
tending to draw others after them, habits soliciting imitation.
Something mysterious plays in this Confucian conviction.
Like the Platonic notion that people will only make a good
society and be what they might be if they are *persuaded* that
the love of wisdom and virtue makes the best life, the Confucian focus on the attractiveness of virtue expresses a deep
faith in human nature. Aristotle, thinking much as Plato had

thought, posited as the foundation of his metaphysics and ethics that all people by nature desire to know. Confucius, less speculative than Aristotle and more interested in the practical virtues, might have said that all people by nature desire to become benevolent.

None of these thinkers was a foolish optimist. All had enough experience of human affairs to know that many people are intellectually and morally slothful. Following up on the desire to know, gaining competence through disciplined study, is hard work. Many fall by the wayside because they are unwilling to perform it. Similarly, taking the notion of benevolence to heart, getting it to root in one's substance so that slowly but steadily one actually becomes benevolent, dominated by a goodness that wants to help others become more human, can become a laborious undertaking. Many fall by the wayside in moral matters, too, preferring quick pleasure to the quieter, paler satisfaction of having done what was right. Despite such lessons from common observation, however, masters such as Aristotle and Confucius continued to think of human nature as fit for philosophy and the gentlemanly life. So the paradox they encountered was the difficulty involved in people's becoming what they were fitted to be, in human beings' only becoming human through much hard work.

Part of the attraction of virtue therefore is the signals it gives that its possessor has triumphed over many a temptation to laziness and self-indulgence. Even when we admit that some people find benevolence easier than others, as some people find logic and metaphysics easier than others, it remains true that virtue strong enough to stand out and be recognized usually witnesses to many admirable victories.

And yet, the masters, the saints, the paragons seldom speak much about the struggles they went through. To their mind, the struggles were nothing compared to the benefits they saw, the love that flared in their hearts. It is somewhat comparable to the struggles of parenting. Considered in the abstract, the demands children make on parents might be enough to persuade those contemplating parenthood that it is likely to be a bad bargain. But when the miracle has happened and a new life has come into one's arms, such calculations vanish like fog before the sun. That too is mysterious. One can say that nature, evolution, has put it in parents' genes to love their offspring and be willing to sacrifice for them, so that the race will go on. One can say that motherhood can become the strongest of passions, leading to sacrifices many accountants could never make tally with balancing gains. But such speech merely shifts the mysteriousness, forcing us to realize that some things are good in themselves. Some things are self-justifying and only reveal their full significance when they are done for their own sake. Raising children, for all its demands or even heartache, is most likely to seem significant, something deeply important to human existence, when it is done for its own sake, putting in the background parental pride, or thoughts of the gains the children might bring, or plans to have the children inherit the business or the house. In the foreground, representing the crux of the matter, should be the give and take between the infant who needs and the parent who needs to be needed, between the teenager who seeks counsel and the parent who wonders what in the world to say, between the young adult able to offer new ideas and strength and the older parent who finally is in a position to proffer some wisdom.

The analogy to education and social service lies in this matter of doing things for their own sake. To structure formal education as a matter of preparing for a job, that one may occupy a niche in the world of work, seriously jars with Aristotle's profound insight into the roots of knowledge. The natural desire to know stretches far beyond what is necessary to earn one's bread. Indeed, unless it ventures into what Aristotelians called "first philosophy," where the questions boil down to an interrogation of the ultimate structures of reality, it will be seriously stunted. This in turn will force the person's whole soul out of shape, leading to either idolatry or apathy about the most important human questions and drives.

Social service should be done for its own sake because it involves similar dynamics. Benevolence, neighborly love, is a call in one's conscience that, rightly interpreted, is not so much a duty as an adventure. There stand other human beings, lacking something important, asking for help. Each is a project much like oneself: a venture in trying to understand the human condition, to cope with its challenges, to take advantage of its opportunities and so transcend one's present limitations, expand one's present horizons. But somehow, to some degree, temporarily or permanently, the project has gone astray. In trying to help another person in need, one learns to be thankful for what has gone right in one's own project and to be humbler about the fragility of all people's lives. There but for an accident of birth, or schooling, or genetics, or the stock market, or color goes oneself. There is another road one could have taken, not all bad but much quite painful. For a moment, one should play the novelist, imagining the twists and turns of such a road. For a moment, one should linger with the insight that none of us control our destiny, each of us has to beg the benevolence of whatever powers set the whole cluster of evolutionary encounters in place.

Take the victims of war. A few of them were prominent players in the interactions that led up to the war, but most were not. Most were people pushed out of shape by forces anonymous others set in motion. How did they happen onto the stage at such an inauspicious moment? Why was it their country, their generation, that became the site of the irreconcilable differences, of the hatreds that stuttered out in the machine gun bullets and launched the bombs? In such grand examples of the passive, patient, suffering side of history as war, we see written large a fact that ordinary, deceptively peaceful existence obscures for most people. This is all that they undergo, all that is out of their hands. This is all that is either providential or absurd, either connected with a Way organizing the cosmic whole or with a massive absurdity.

The virtue attractive in face of such a view of history and personal experience is a trust similar to Aristotle's trust in the desire to know and Master Kung's trust in the good effects good character has on others. One has to trust that education, social service, peacemaking, trying to right wrong relations, and all the rest are factors in what is finally a trustable whole. In fact, thinking that education, working for justice, and the rest are worthwhile, keeping at them even through the dark days when human perversity says they are useless, is tantamount to trusting in the goodness, the meaningfulness, of the entire cosmic venture. The sages, East and West, all inculcate such trust. Without saying that ours is the best of worlds, or denying that human beings regularly are perverse, their smiles, their auras of peace, witness to the self-validating power of what they have seen and tried to pass on. Confucius was attracted to the virtue of the sages of yore, so he tried to understand it, appropriate it, and pass it on. What are the virtues to which we are attracted? How does benevolence, or human greatness, or admirable social service shine in our sight? What could it do for our lives, with which no doubt we are less than fully satisfied at present, to probe such attractive virtues, put out some effort to understand them, try them on as garments that might fit ourselves? When we start to ask such questions, we venture on the possibility of discipleship: of saying there is something we'd like to believe in, there is a master or mistress we'd love to follow and imitate.

7:8: DESIRE

"The Master said, 'I never enlighten anyone who has not been driven to distraction by trying to understand a difficulty or who has not got into a frenzy trying to put his ideas into words. When I have pointed out one corner of a square to anyone and he does not come back with the other three, I will not point it out to him a second time.' "

Because of his convictions about the naturalness of benevolence, and so of the striving to acquire it through education, the Master was hard on his disciples. Like a Zen master, he wanted constant signs that the disciple was striving with might and main to understand, to gain enlightenment. Thus we come upon a second aspect of desire, where the goal is not something that will keep one in samsara or, in Confucian terms, something that will compound one's problems in securing benevolence but something that will spring one free of ignorance and vice.

All people by nature desire to know, but not all people feel this desire, treasure it, and move it to the center of their motivation. Each day teachers looking out at a class instinctively divide the group into the sheep and the goats: those who are there to a purpose, who have a hunger to learn, and those who are spinning their wheels, wasting everyone's time. Many teachers have the experience that their most rewarding students are those who are older, have struggled with family life and work, and therefore have come back to college with a strong will to learn. Until students do have a strong will to learn, they are not likely to grasp what all the fuss is about. Until they feel ignorant, and so diminished, frustrated, one has little leverage with them. Exams, grades, papers, and all the rest are only so much baggage, so many bootless rituals, until students and teachers alike see them as means of exciting, disciplining, and rewarding the desire to know.

So Master Kung wanted students who had been driven to distraction trying to understand a supposedly important passage in one of the classics, or trying to solve a practical dilemma in political affairs. He required that people have a head of steam up, be fully involved in their studies. And if he gave a student a lead only to find it was not followed up, he consigned that student to the dustbin. How many of us, or of our students, could pass such a rigorous exam? Is education much less effective, much less serious, than it might be because we have grown afraid to require that students and teachers be passionate about it? Perhaps it would be better for all involved if we quartered the number of students and faculty involved, leaving only those who were there solely to learn. That is a quixotic proposal, of course, but the poignancy it raises is instructive.

In philosophy, political science, religious studies, literature, history, and other humanistic studies, the classics one treats usually are works of passion. The writers we most hymn—Plato, Aristotle, Lao Tzu, Dante, Thucydides—were intensely involved in their work and thought it important to the survival of humanity as they reverenced it. For some good reasons, and more bad reasons, we have contrived to hold such classical authors at arm's length. The same with our typical treatment of Confucius. Beneath Master Kung's sober, sometimes quite cynical sayings beats the heart of a man stirred to propose a revolution. In place of the disastrous, feckless reliance on power-plays in his day he wanted to establish rulers who knew how reality held together, who honored the great traditions of the past, who realized the people were a trust placed in their hands as a mandate from Heaven. In place of the venal, stupid, self-serving types who slashed at the common weal through smallness of soul, he wanted to establish people of substance, people who loved what was right with little concern for the advantages it might bring them. And this great effort was the passion of the Master's life, the cause for which he lived. Like Jesus with his gospel about the Kingdom of God, or the Buddha with his Dharma, Confucius wanted to change the world, to remake human beings so that their potential might finally flower.

Of course, we in are in a position to realize that passion can become fanaticism, all the more so when it calls itself passion for God or ultimate wisdom. But none of the heroes we have mentioned were fanatics, people passionate on the model of our latter-day bigots who think murder the way the deity would transform creation. Their passionate pursuit of wisdom held its own correctives. Because they wanted to know what was real, how people in fact were constituted and tended to behave, why silence so frequently was more appropriate than speech, such masters learned to stop their mouths, tamp down their fire, wait on the proper moment when finally their audience might be ready to take their words to heart.

There is a time to speak and a time to keep silence. There is a time to propose peace and justice as the marrow of human well-being and a time to fear that making such a proposal will only bring work for peace and justice into further contempt. On the one hand, one must preach one's gospel, one's good news about what benevolence or detachment can accomplish, in season and out of season. On the other hand, one must be as wise as the serpent that doesn't bother with unattainable targets, as innocent as the dove that broods life in the more favorable nest. Confucian courage caused the Master to reject everything ignoble and send packing students not burning to learn. Confucian prudence caused the Master to work out a balanced theory, one that paid proper honor to both the stove and high Heaven. The docility that the great masters have asked of their students has been but a reflection of the docility they have tried to offer their God, their conscience, their own model teachers. Socrates listening to his daimon is like Confucius trying to keep faith with the wise leaders of yore. The Buddha risking all on the value of enlightenment is like Jesus risking all on obedience to his heavenly Father. Great education and great contributions to peace and justice both depend on such obedience, such enlightenment, such docility. Amazingly enough, the most fearless champions of freedom have been the masters who moved might and main to hear the voice of Truth as a still small voice at the fine point of their soul. Gandhi comes to mind, but he has myriad brothers and sisters. Discernment, as religious people tend to call it, is the hallmark of those who want to serve the Truth rather than expediency, God rather than mammon. They are the peacemakers, the just, the people who make the real difference.

The majority of them are not famous. The majority are ordinary citizens, workers on the line, who quietly say no to wrong compromises, quietly insist that they will not accept cant, jingoism, faulty reasoning and faulty motives. They shame the rest of us, who are not eager for virtue, don't follow up on the lessons they and the great books have offered us. But as long as they stick to their posts, alert and unflinching, we still have a cloud of witnesses persuading us that it is possible, conscience does make a difference, the spiritual life is not an illusion but the realest thing about us. God bless them every one.

Discussion Questions

1. What have the followers of Confucius understand by *jen* and *li?*

2. How would benevolence and proper ritualism coincide in an ideal celebration of Christmas or the Fourth of July?

3. Why have so many traditions associated Heaven with the source of light, wisdom, and the sanction for their customs?

4. How valid is a description that contrasts the secular and the religious souls as closed and open?

5. Why did the Master make so much of mourning properly?

6. How does tolerance correlate with a profound grasp of essentials?

7. Why is the wise person immunized against exultation at wealth and depression at poverty?

8. How can poverty both suppress one's humanity and aid it?

9. What in human nature makes virtue attractive?

10. What in human nature makes virtue unattractive?

11. How should teachers or spiritual instructors insist that their students be passionate about learning?

12. Why is docility to the truth or the voice of conscience so characteristic a feature of the great religious masters?

Notes

1. See Herbert Fingarette, *Confucius—the Secular as Sacred* (New York: Harper & Row, 1972). On Confucianism in general see Wing-Tsit Chan, "Confucian Thought: Foundations of the Tradition," ER, vol. 4, pp. 15–24; Lawrence G. Thompson, *The Chinese Religion: An Introduction* (Belmont, Calif.: Wadsworth, 1979); Marcel Granet, *The Religion of the Chinese People* (New York: Harper Torchbooks, 1975); C.K. Yang, *Religion in Chinese Society* (Berkeley: University of California Press, 1970); Donald G. Munro, *The Concept of Man in Early China* (Stanford, Calif.: Stanford University Press, 1969).

2. All translations are from *Confucius: The Analects,* trans. D.C. Lau (New York: Penguin, 1979).

Chapter 5

TAOISM AND THE TAO TE CHING

THE TAOIST WORLDVIEW

Most scholars consider Lao Tzu, the author traditionally credited with having written the *Tao Te Ching* and thereby founded Taoism, a mythical figure. The Tao Te Ching (*The Way and its Power*) apparently was circulating two centuries after Confucius and the Analects, and the traditional date of the death of Lao Tzu was 520 B.C.E., which would have made him an older contemporary of Confucius. Indeed, legends had him besting Confucius in debate. The historical reality is probably that various masters contributed to this short but very influential text, which has owed its popularity to its obscurity as much as its depth.

"In office, a Confucian, in retirement, a Taoist" has been the well-worn slogan summarizing the relationship between Confucianism and Taoism. Confucianism fit the official, bureaucratic needs of imperial China. It stressed order, hierarchy, discipline, inner goodness, and outer punctiliousness. It was conservative, traditional, an outlook calculated to bring up submissive women, devoted children, obedient subjects. Taoism also claimed to be traditional, but the tradition it represented was wilder, more poetic, suspicious of social organization, convinced that the best life was the life closest to nature. The Tao the followers of Lao Tzu and Chuang Tzu (another influential writer) revered was the Way coursing through nature. As we shall see, they thought nature both

96

careless of human affairs and indirect, subtle, as most human leaders were too stupid to be.

Nature obviously was careless of human beings, treating them like the straw dogs used in the sacrifices, because storm and flood came with little regard for human feelings. Infants died, stabbing at their parents' hearts. Golden days came without warning, forcing people to smile and renew their hope. And all of this went on with no fuss, no psychology. Nature had no conscience, no subjectivity. Therefore the Taoist, the person trying to gain harmony with nature, was shaped toward objectivity. Chuang Tzu, for example, mocked those who ostentatiously mourned the death of their parents or friends. To his mind death was natural, part of the Great Clod's persistent turning. The Great Clod, nature, had brought one into life, where one had taken nourishment from other creatures and used them for one's survival. Was it not fitting that the Great Clod one day should put one back into the ground, ask one to repay one's debts by becoming fertilizer? So when Chuang Tzu's wife died he defied convention, singing and drumming. What he had had with her was good, but now a new phase had come for both of them. If they had praised nature for the good times, ought they not to accept death and transition?[1]

The Way moving through nature also was indirect, subtle, and relentlessly effective as few human rulers had the wit to be. Nature regularly moved by what the Taoists called *wu-wei,* not-doing, actionless action or creative passivity. Women knew this better than men, moving men who were physically and socially more powerful than they by charm, patience, suggestion. Infants instinctively wrapped the household around their little fingers, making their helplessness an attractive tyranny. If you wanted to accomplish things as nature did, surely and steadily, you had to apprentice yourself to the water that wears away rock, to the valley that survives storms better than the mountain, to the gnarled, ugly tree that stands long after the straight, handsome tree has been cut down for furniture.

This entailed a new angle of vision, a shift of perspective, as all significant religious or philosophical conversions do. It meant looking at a room and giving more significance to the space in it than to the walls and furniture. Most people credit the walls and the furniture with making the room attractive, habitable, useful. But in fact it is the space they enclose and adorn that makes a room significant. Moving through such space, sharing it, working in it, people accomplish their lives. The walls and furniture are incidental, things in the order of means to the end of enjoying a serviceable space.

The Taoists implied that such a way of looking at nature and human beings' place in it predominated before social conventions and laws multiplied to help human beings lose themselves in culture. No doubt this was a romantic and naive view, but it fueled the Taoist conviction that the best life is simple, plain, even rude. Better the days when people ate simple, rough, but tasty and satisfying food than these latter days when *haute cuisine* made everything dainty and unnourishing. Better the days when people worked with their hands, knew the soil and the elements intimately, than these latter days when so many pushed paper, worked on words. In the old days people had few wants and many satisfactions. In these latter days people multiplied wants and could barely get a good night's sleep. The Taoists wanted vigorous, energetic, solid lives that people enjoyed with animal satisfaction. They wanted leisure in which to turn with the seasons, ease in which to let their spirits soar that they might ride the wind of imagination, follow the outreach of the ecstatic spirit for blank intercourse with the Great Clod as a whole. As Confucianism tended to make a busy, talky sort of life, so then-modern technology tended to interpose itself between people and nature, depleting their vigor, preoccupying their time.

Part of the Taoist program therefore was a call to get back to the basics. In perhaps the most important figure of the Tao Te Ching, Lao Tzu urged respect for the uncarved block—human nature prior to its being worked on by social conventions, human nature when it was simple, whole, full of potential. The Taoists constantly criticized "higher" culture for the price it exacted. Abuzz with ideas and projects, people were losing touch with the earth, forgetting their roots, attenuating their embodied existence. That was not how the Tao ran the rest of creation. It ill fit human beings' animality, the wisdoms of the flesh. To live a long, contented life, one not only had to come to grips with these wisdoms but to honor them. Rushing around, worrying, spilling oneself out in talk and projects would only bring angina and shaky nerves. Going with the grain of nature, letting the earth and the sky, the sun and the rain, work on one through the seasons would bring harmony, peace. What would be would be. The wisest human beings took themselves apart from the vagaries of human affairs, the irrational shifts of the economy and polity, of the social scene and the world of fashion, of the schools that changed their curricula as though they were shirts. In retirement, cultivating their spirits and their plot of soil, wise people let nature be the source of their wealth, their freedom, their sense of place, their feeling of beauty, their wisdom about the beginning and the beyond.

Not surprisingly, the political thrust of the Tao Te Ching ran towards simplicity. The best government was the least government. The best law was the fewest rules. Indeed, as laws multiplied so did criminals. If you wanted to decrease the criminal population, you ought to strike most of the laws from the books. The wise ruler worked as though frying fish: as little stirring as possible. The shrewd, effective ruler kept the people ignorant, so that their desires would remain few. Give people ideas, fill them with desires, and soon you would be harvesting discontent. The way to peace was to help people accept their lot, achieve a quiet, plain life pivoted on satisfying work, satisfying thought (contemplation), satisfying food, sex, children, clothing, friends. Lao Tzu was so impressed by the vastness and subtlety of nature, and so distressed by the folly of human affairs, that his constant refrain was "back to the

Tao." The Way of nature, piping through the ten thousand things of creation, was the path to peace. What justice human beings could achieve boiled down to accepting the treatment an objective, dispassionate nature dispensed. Take people away from their artificiality, back toward their uncarved blocks, and you would improve most people's lot. Bring them closer to the Tao and you would give them the most justice they could hope to receive.

8/20, 22: WATER

"Highest good is like water. Because water excels in benefiting the myriad creatures without contending with them and settles where none would like to be, it comes close to the way.
"It is because it does not contend that it is never at fault."[2]

Here we have the figure of water mentioned in the previous section. The highest good is the sort of effect produced by the Tao: order untainted by human fussiness. Lao Tzu marvels at the *wu-wei* of water. It does not contend, will not fight for its rights. In his day, as in the day of Confucius, the problem was too much contention. Most rulers and would-be rulers thought the way to power (for the sake of the common good, of course) was to use force (*pa*). Confucius thought only the force of virtue could get done the job that really needed doing. Lao Tzu was even more radical. For him the most effective power was that which calls no attention to itself, which slips through the nets of contention. Water benefits all living things, yet it does not shout about its benefactions or hoist billboards. (Lao Tzu is forgetting storms and floods.) It offers little resistance (in matters of small scale) to those who want to shunt it one way or another. It is the antithesis of the egomaniacs who are always pushing their causes, always trying to impose their will. Yet look at what water accomplishes: nourishment for plants, animals, and human beings; relief from debilitating heat; cleansing; delight to the eye when the sun dances on its surface.

Settling where none would like to be, taking the lowest place and slipping through the mossy cracks, water gives object lessons in humility and objectivity. It does what it has to do, not grousing about where that takes it. It wears down the opposition by persistence, shows utmost flexibility, can even change its state when the going gets too hot or too cold. In all this it comes close to, is neighbor to, mirror of, the Way that runs creation. The Way is if anything less visible, less prominent than water. Most people seldom notice its action, seldom realize its necessity. Yet Lao Tzu assumed something had to be running the world, had to account for natural order. And most likely he felt he had communed with this something when he had slipped the moorings of his workaday mind and let his spirit wander the four directions. Moreover, tradition had long spoken of the Way—the path followed by the ancients so loved by Confucius, and the path prescribed by high Heaven, which oversaw all. So there were historical, empirical, and philosophical grounds for thinking the Way a solid reality. If one was aware of such quiet but massively significant operations as erosion, the shifting of the temperatures, the movement of the stars, and the drift of the popular will, one had plenty of stimuli for thinking deeply and correctly about the Tao.

The final line, which says that because it does not contend it (water or the Tao) is never at fault, is the most provocative. For, first, it overlooks the "contentions" of water when it turns destructive and of the Tao when it wears people down through sickness or accident. And, second, it implies that the more human beings imitate these models in not contending the less faulty human beings will be. Fault, in the sense of being responsible for social upset, comes from striving, wanting, proposing, being aggressive. Fault, in the sense of

101

having a flaw in one's makeup, sand in one's gears, comes from losing the harmony there should be between matter and spirit, between the entire human being and the Tao, by ceasing to listen to the music of the spheres.

Now, Lao Tzu is playing a slick game, because he has purposes for his writing. He wants not only to express what he has experienced and thought, what he has come to think true, but also to change people's minds. Indeed, he wants to change enough minds to shift Chinese culture away from the way it has recently been doing business. So he is in fact contending with the status quo. The Confucians, and others who do not accept his radical sense of the Tao, are his enemies. The Tao Te Ching might even be called a polemical work, a salvo in a philosophical war. Yet, to his credit, Lao Tzu generally chooses a form that exemplifies his content. Although in fact he is promoting his point of view, in manner he is detached, objective, egoless (anonymous)—simply doing poetic philosophy the way a lawn sends up dandelions, the way a toddler strews chaos.

Is this advocacy of not contending, or working through *wu-wei,* the same as Indian non-violence? Yes and no. Analytically, the two concepts seem quite close. Both imply detachment, selflessness, taming desire, not entering the samsaric fray. Psychologically, they probably stem from similar, cousinly experiences: the peace that comes from detachment, the relief that shifting from hot emotions to cool can bring. But culturally and socially they diverge, because Indian and Chinese cultures generally have diverged. Where India has been abstract, speculative, tempted to a matter/spirit dichotomy, China has been concrete, practical, holistic. Thus Chinese *wu-wei* remains closer to the fray than Indian *ahimsa.* The Hindu or Buddhist ascetic retires to the forest, while the Taoist just goes to the country. Both despise war, but an Arjuna has a rationale for participating in war without granting it much significance. A Lao Tzu is more interested in undercutting war, defusing violence, teaching people to get their decent way by sleight of hand and obscurity.

What fills the souls and days of people who think they should avoid contention? If they are not going to push and pull with the bully-boys, what are they going to do? Not cut out paper dolls. Lao Tzu is not advocating recreation on the order of children's games or therapy for those whose sense has gone south. He is advocating a private life attuned to the Tao, a life of contemplation or even mysticism, and a public life that gambles on being nimbler than one's opposition, able to score points, perhaps even win the game, by being quicker and smarter. The Taoist wants to man the skill positions, without most people knowing he is doing so. She wants to be the power behind the throne, since the throne is off-limits to her sex (and usually more a burden than a benefit anyway).

All of this suggests a whimsical, sportive personality, someone for whom private life might be an art-work and public life might be a serious game. Not taking on the burdens of the sober-sided Confucians, a Chuang Tzu could set up as a gadfly, a crank. There is a further question, of course, concerning what would happen if all people, or just all talented people, turned into gadflies and cranks, but Chuang Tzu might well have pointed out that in most times and places there are plenty of earnest types all too happy to take up the white man's burden. Until the day came when poetic philosophers could be princes, because the populace wanted wit and depth at the top, playing the gadfly would remain a noble, socratic vocation.

The Taoist therefore could be akin to the satirist, the cartoonist, the artist whose new, apparently distorting angle on the ordinary makes us think about the ordinary more profoundly than we had hitherto. All are lively spirits skating on thin ice between humor and despair. The pretentiousness of people prompts laughter. The obtuseness and destructiveness of people prompt despair. Between the two moves the Tao

103

that is serene because more comprehensive than human affairs and less vulnerable. The Taoist will only find the art and satiric spirit necessary to make public life adventurous by finding the path the Tao has cleared, just as the Christian will only find the means to call existence a divine comedy when taken over by the Holy Spirit. Both are wise to seem not to contend, because on the level of power-plays both are bound to be crushed. Both play a dangerous game, and never find a zone fully fault-free, because both in fact are contending—for the sanity, perspective, order that only come when one has an open soul. Witnessing to right order, Lao Tzu witnesses to the very source, the actual logos, of peace and justice alike. More human than the Tao, he cannot avoid taking sides, hoping to bring people to their senses and save them from more pain.

15/35: SUBTLETY

"Of old he who was well versed in the way was minutely subtle, mysteriously comprehending, and too profound to be known. It is because he could not be known that he can only be given a makeshift description: tentative, as if fording a river in winter, hesitant, as if in fear of his neighbors; formal like a guest; falling apart like thawing ice; thick like the uncarved block; vacant like a valley; murky like muddy water."

This tantalizing verse piles up descriptions of the ideal Taoist, the person moving in the Way. Note, first, that Lao Tzu places this person in the deep past: "of old." The implication is that things were better way back then. Many cultures have myths of a golden age. It is a regular tendency of religions to think that in pristine times holiness flourished and since then things have gone downhill. Even Christian enthusiasm for the apostolic age, the New Testament era, partakes of this tendency. In Lao Tzu, as we have seen, it came in part as a reaction to present times, which were out of joint. Probably much the same happens in other instances of nostalgia, other projections of an "in the beginning things were better." The times almost always are out of joint. Consequently, beginnings almost always seem to have had greener grass. Perhaps religious maturation involves coming to read such archaism as a projection of psychic need, and so to balance one's judgments of what actually occurred, what the historical actuality was, with an appreciation of the symbolic value pristine beginnings seem bound to acquire.

At any rate, the Taoist hero classically was subtle and alert to small things, most likely because he sensed the Tao played in the rustle of leaves as well as in battles, in the babble of children as well as the pyrotechnics of thunder and lightning. As well the hero was "mysteriously comprehending," an enigmatic phrase worth ruminating upon. It could mean he knew things without showing how, or maybe even without knowing how. It could also mean he was comprehensive in his outreach, took the full span of reality for his province. Either way, what he knew and what he covered had something haunting, deep, impenetrable about them. From his intimacy with the Tao he had taken on some of the Tao's opacity. Therefore, one's best approach to him came by simply appreciating what he was, not by trying to analyze his every word or motion. He was a whole, as the Tao was a whole, and so he could only be grasped holistically. That is somewhat true of all people, since all have depths and quirks no other human being will ever master. But in the case of the Taoist hero the depths and quirks were of striking quality. Unless one at least sensed what the Tao could make of a docile spirit, one would never come close to getting him in perspective.

Because the great Taoist of old was too deep to be known, one could only strike off aspects of his being, using vivid but failing similes. He was tentative, like one carefully making his way across a river in winter, not sure how long the ice would hold or afraid the water rushing over the rocks would tip him over. Life did not lie before him as an obvious, easy enterprise. He was not like the cocksure pragmatic types who saw no mystery and barely tolerated puzzles. If their world often became a flatland, his world had at least four dimensions, maybe more. The deeper one has been taken into the creative mystery, the less cocksure one becomes. Thus Socrates, at the peak of his wisdom, summarized his achievement as knowing that he did not know. Thus Aquinas, having been taken to mystical experience of the divinity, felt all the tomes he previously had written were so much straw. The fullness of reality so overspills the little container of our minds that whenever the heavens open to suggest its extent people feel they have gone deaf and dumb. They have no words with which to describe the simple, dazzling whole, and the words they used to employ, like the words others continue to push at them, no longer carry. So they are tentative about charting the mystery, leading a march across the stream of existence (an important Buddhist figure: nirvana is on the far side of this stream; the ultimate wisdom is that which has "gone beyond"). In fact this seldom keeps religious saints from acting vigorously, but it makes their judgments modest and their personal claims instructively few. They tend to move by an instinct that gives them considerable certitude but which they find hard to articulate as principles others could apply without fail.

The Taoist hero is not merely tentative, hesitant, but also formal. He dislikes easy familiarity, wants to imitate the objectivity of the Tao and not fall into the false intimacy exhibited by many subjectivists. Were we speaking of Confucians, we might say that the master is formal because he knows his superior place in the hierarchy and insists on his rights. The Taoist atmosphere does not prompt such a hierarchical or prickly figure. The Taoist sage may be abrupt, rude, unwilling to suffer fools, but if so it is not because he thinks well of himself and wants to be sure the hierarchical system that ranks him high stays in place. If he is formal it is because he wants to respect the mysteriousness of other people and each new situation into which he comes. The world is full of wonders. Each day is a new creation. So he feels called to respect it, reverence it, not barge in. He could well be a patron saint for ecologists.

What it means for the Taoist sage to fall apart like thawing ice is unclear. Perhaps being in the Tao has melted much of his prior molding, has caused his personality to liquify and flow like the Tao itself. The figure of the uncarved block should bring to mind all we said previously about Lao Tzu's preference for human nature before it got worked over by higher culture. To be vacant like a valley could be to be waiting to be filled. Perhaps the sage wanted to let the Tao move through him like wind, snow, rain, the clouds that cause shifting patterns of shadows. To be murky like muddy water is reminiscent of the way many mystics talk. Having been overshadowed by the divine reality, they find their previous clarity about human affairs has deserted them. They are confused, feel stupid, wonder if they can still function. The assumptions of the crowd seem to them more than passing strange, maybe even crazy. So the Buddha, having finally seen death, disease, and old age, left the castle where he had been living a pampered life and sought enlightenment, marveling that any people could foresee their dismal future (in death, disease, and old age) and not be galvanized into trying to defeat it. So Jesus prayed that his Father would forgive those crucifying him, because they didn't know what they were doing.

Do people going to war know what they are doing? Do people pulling the levers of an unjust economic system, or a political system that marginalizes huge numbers, or a church that discrimates against women, or a country that practices apartheid, or a religio-political group that hates Jews—do any of these know what they are doing? The person who has gone into the cloud of unknowing, been immersed in the muddy water of the Tao, finds them demented. In their hyperclarity, their simplicism, their know-nothing assurance they appear mentally ill. If the world, reality, is as God, the Tao, the Buddhanature show it to be, they are literally in-sane, sick in mind and soul. This may be more the fault of their culture than that of their own choices, but as they stand they can seem representatives of a different, inhuman species. Slowly, then, the mystic must remember whence he or she came, what things were like prior to enlightenment, and what stories might entice the warmakers, the criminals, the spiritually obtuse into the yearning for peace that gives the Tao access to them. Slowly, all of us must learn that only the experience of the whole can heal such people of their partiality, their idiosyncrasy, their destructiveness.

18/42: DECLINE

"When the great way falls into disuse there are benevolence and rectitude; when cleverness emerges there is great hypocrisy; when the six relations are at variance there are filial children; when the state is benighted there are loyal ministers."

This verse is one of Lao Tzu's sharpest attacks on the Confucians. Throughout, he characterizes their virtues, their sense of good order, as a devolution from the straightforward, natural goodness that prevailed when the Tao held full sway. The Tao is the great way, the path the cosmos follows and human beings miss at their peril. To walk in the great way is to imitate nature in being what one is, doing what one has to do, unselfconsciously, easily. Does a tiger think about the hunt? Do the birds file flight plans? Zen Buddhists, who were much influenced by Taoism, often used nature to symbolize the instinctive wholeness of the Buddhanature. Let the Buddhanature emerge and one would overcome the dichotomies between mind and spirit, would oust the dualistic thinking that keeps people from living harmoniously. In the Taoists' own terms, the goal was to act with "no mind." Thus the ideal calligrapher simply dipped in her pen and let the ideographs flow. The accomplished poet simply opened his mouth and let the verses pour out. Pottery, the martial arts, acrobatics, and even government all ought to have come naturally, as an expression of a core self immersed in the Tao, at one with nature.

Against this background, talk about benevolence and rectitude (*jen, li,* and the other Confucian virtues) witnessed to a decline. People now had to analyze, plan, discuss what once had been spontaneous. Lao Tzu may be naive about the historical past, or deliberately misconstruing it to make a point, but his psychological portrait is fascinating. Part of his insight recalls Aquinas' statement that the wise person doesn't worry much about names. What we call a virtue or insight matters far less than our possessing the virtue or having the act of understanding. Another part recalls the experience of having had to leave a reality in order to name and analyze it. For example, an artist has to step back, shift gears, take up a new mental focus to become an art critic. An athlete has to leave the flow of the game to become a commentator on technique. Although Lao Tzu is not giving the significance of such shifts, such acts of detachment and analysis, their due, he makes a point all performers will appreciate. The fully creative moment is one of immersion. Whether it's the poet chasing the images as they arise fresh from the subconscious, or the swimmer riding high in the water at a time of perfect synchronicity, or the politician feeling consensus build and guiding it dexterously, in most instances of significant creativity the worker is one with the materials, the environment. Because of such fusion or immersion, hundreds of subtle, even ineffable bits of understanding are in play. One feels them more than one thinks about them. One hasn't the time to name or judge them, because that isn't the point. The point is interacting with one's material, moving one's fellow workers, keeping the work, the mood, the process building. Later one can reflect on the process, take a detached look at the product, revisit the empty theater or the ballpark to analyze what occurred. Such second, subsequent moments are extremely valuable, because creativity usually requires refinement and criticism if it is to continue to grow. Nonetheless, the subsequent, critical moments should be for the sake of future prior, immersed, creative moments. The creative work is the whole, the treasure, while the analytical work is merely the part, the servant charged with polishing the treasure.

If one stereotypes Lao Tzu and Confucius, Lao Tzu is the artist, concerned with performing the Taoist dance. Confucius is the critic, concerned with analyzing how Chinese culture might be better ordered. This is a stereotype, because both masters deal with both performance and critique. But Lao Tzu has the stronger sense of what it is like to be in the magic, mystical moment. Lao Tzu is closer to, more driven by, the ineffable experience of union.

The other comments of the verse depend on this contrast between the magic moment of full creativity, the blessed time when humanity actually obtains, and the subsequent time of dissection and prescription.[3] In the depths of the Tao, there is not cleverness, but opacity, as we have seen. To be in the horizon of cleverness, of the mind that carves things up like a sharp knife, one has to have left the mystic's wholeness and muteness. The mystic's mind tends to be in neutral or free-fall. For the mystic the heart, the center of the self, is the crux. Loving from this center, reaching out to embrace the godhead or the Tao that it might fill every pore, the mystic lets the mind whirl as it will, paying it little heed. In the past the mind has never led to full union with the Tao, so when the Tao actually is sensed the mind can seem irrelevant, even dangerous. To be sure, the highly developed mystical traditions give the mind rights and insist that inspiration or enthusiasm not take people to irrational doctrines or actions. But this again concerns subsequent, secondary matters. When one actually is united with the Tao there is no cleverness, so when there is cleverness one is out of full union.

On their own terms and plane of consciousness, clever people are not necessary hypocritical. They only become hypocritical when their cleverness leads them to separate what they know and say from what they do. Hypocrisy is the mismatch between one's persona, what one professes to be, and how one actually behaves, how one speaks to divinity at midnight, when the crowds have departed. Still, even to be on the plane of such a need to match persona and real self is to be out of union with the Tao.

The six relations are those between parent and child, husband and wife, elder siblings and younger siblings. Each of the three connections is a two-way street, yielding six different points of view. Lao Tzu thinks these relations are so natural that people only talk about them when something has gone wrong. Thus there would be no discussion of the filial child were there not sons and daughters failing to respect their parents. It is a bit like the appearance of a new disease. Twenty years ago there was no discussion of AIDS because the physiological disorders comprising AIDS were not occurring as they recently have been. To Lao Tzu's mind an unfilial relation was a disorder, a disease, that simply would not have been available to provoke comment had the Tao not fallen into disuse.

The same with the final comment dealing with the benighted state and loyal ministers. To have to discourse on statecraft already suggests a time of decline, a fall from grace. One could debate whether there ever had been an unfallen Chinese state, but that would be to miss Lao Tzu's point. He is concerned with what harmony with the Tao shows genuine human being to be like. Because harmony with the Tao is so rare, in its light business as usual, even the business of clarifying virtue and statecraft by an intelligence as venerable as that of Confucius, is bound to seem common (nothing precious) or even downright ugly.

In the West we have said that grace perfects nature. For Taoists the translation might be, the experience of the Tao takes people to states that reveal what domestic and civil life ought to be. West and East, the people talking from experience of ultimate reality have been bound to think the solution to human disorder—domestic violence, warfare, avoidable poverty, discrimination—lay in ushering people into the contact with ultimate reality that might transform them.[4] Without such transformation, such grace, the mystics have seen little chance that people would change their destructive ways. That is why they have made prayer—contemplation—a political act. One can't do for others what one has not oneself become. We won't have the peaceful, just social life we want until we have been remade to the core.

19/43a: PLAINNESS

" . . . the people must have something to which they can attach themselves: Exhibit the unadorned and embrace the uncarved block, have little thought of self and as few desires as possible."

We read this text as akin to the conviction of the last text that transformative contact with the Tao is the way to reset human nature so that decent common life might become possible. In the first lines of this text, Lao Tzu has criticized Confucian or commonsensical virtues as he had done in the prior text: do away with the "sage," discard the "wise," exterminate "benevolence," throw away "rectitude," get rid of "ingenuity" and "profit." All of these terms are bourgeois. All bespeak a narrowed soul that has lost the wonder and fullness that immersion in the Tao would have provided. The sage could descend to being someone who knew the ritual protocols. The wise person could be someone merely shrewd enough to have survived to a wizened old age. Benevolence could be the easy charity of the rich person sitting atop a pile of ill-gotten wealth. Rectitude could be the hallmark of busy puritans, people so unimaginative it never had crossed their minds to question custom. Ingenuity could be the cleverness we castigated in the last section. And profit—what heaps of wrongdoing or misguidance could that name not hide?

No, the people require something simpler, deeper, more stable, realer than these partial terms, ideas, realities. They need something to which they can attach their deepest hopes, their hunger and thirst for being, righteousness, harmony. What could be their rock and salvation, giving them the confidence that they need not fear? What would they find if one could lead them below Confucian propriety, could show them the oceanic Tao? The final lines of the text suggest Lao Tzu's positive response to these questions he has implied.

The unadorned is that which has not been outfitted with high culture. It is the body before people have rigged it out in fashionable clothing. Think of the ages when fashionable clothing, both men's and women's, has kept people tied up and sweating. Think of women's dress shoes. Something healthy, vigorous, beautiful by a more defensible standard has been lost. Adornment, decoration, has become the enemy of ease, health, and performance. The same with food. Think of the price people now pay for elegant meals. Think of the chemicals added to most of the foods one takes home in packages. Think of the fast foods that manage to assault both taste and health. If this is adornment, supposed betterment, back to rice and beans. After two weeks for weaning the system away from what had been poisioning it, rice and beans can taste wonderful. After a month aerobic exercise can make one addicted to health. The bodily wisdoms involved in a Taoist analysis of clothing and food have their psychological analogues. Give up compulsive talking and when you've come through withdrawal you may feel quiet nourishing your soul. Give up rock music and when you've come through withdrawal Vivaldi, Bach, Mozart, and Beethoven may take you worlds away.

True enough, such classical music is quite adorned. But it built on such simpler musical genius as that behind Gregorian chant, and once one has ears to hear its main delights are the simple, haunting melodies all its sophistication sets off.

For Lao Tzu, the unadorned is not the dull or the insipid. It is the healthy, the vigorous, the whole. And in his view such comparisons as those we have been suggesting are not simply a matter of taste. He was not a relativist, anymore than he was an absolutist on the model of Confucian orthodoxy. He was a mystic, a person who had met the depths, the fullness, and come away healed. From his experience he intuited an objective order, furnished by the Tao. The music of the Tao was the melody of health, and human melodies edified, were helpful, in the measure they harmonized with the Tao. In the measure they were cacophonous, unruly, bringers of sensual grossness, enemies of contemplation, they were hateful.

When one embraces the uncarved block, one opens one's soul beyond what carved, narrowed cultural achievements require. This offers the possibility of one's receiving from on high the order, the measure, that makes for personal and social health. The people long for this measure, whether they realize it or not. Instinctively, they know that it would be good measure, pressed down and overflowing. This is especially true if they are people who have good souls but cannot compete with clever types whose minds are more in fashion. It is especially true if they are people living in poverty, people put down by current judgments of social acceptability, people of the wrong color, age, or sex to be in the running for prestige or power. All such people yearn in their marrow for a revolution, a new state of affairs. Many are desperate for a messiah, a kingdom of God, a millennium—three symbols for the new creation they know would be necessary to achieve a just state of affairs.

The last lines of this text move in a Buddhist direction, away from the messianic direction we have just sketched. Taoists have little thought of self because most of their thought goes out to the Tao, where it turns blank and round. They have few desires, because their desires have become one great, undivided longing for union with the Tao. Paradoxically, this has put their feet on the ground. It has knitted their bones and helped them sleep soundly. Open to heaven, they have become better lovers of the earth and the flesh. Fulfilled by heaven, the earth, and their flesh, they have almost without thinking dropped their desires for adornments, success, advancement, wealth, high station. The goods that Confucius acknowledged all people desire are questionable for Taoists such as Lao Tzu. For him wealth is the richness of experience that comes when one is looking and feeling under the inspiration of the Tao. For him high station is being rapt into the heavens or sent over the sea in spiritual exultation. And the economic wonder, the political utility, of this sort of wealth and high station is that it is open to all. It costs little if anything in terms of money. It leads to no power-plays, no backroom struggles. The coin in which it trades can be multiplied without inflating the base coin of the realm. It is free and self-validating, giving formal teachers only minimal employment and requiring no new taxes.

But what would happen to progress, material improvement, scientific development, commercial enterprise, and the other watchwords of modernity if the Taoist mentality became popular? Would what we have most prized for three centuries not come grinding to a halt? Maybe yes, maybe no, but in a Taoist horizon those are not first-order questions. The first-order question is what makes for order, what is fundamentally real, what offers grounding and bedrock satisfaction. The Taoist answer is harmony with the Tao. Of course Taoists needed food, drink, shelter. Of course they wanted to learn, to make beautiful things, to see lovely patterns, to hear soul-stirring sounds. Certainly they wanted healthy children, satisfying love, reliable friends. But they knew that all these wants came into best focus and had the best chance of being met if their souls were peaceful and their heads set on straight.

They surely would die, so they wanted to live long and fully. They surely would remain ignorant of many things, so they wanted to be certain they had learned the essentials, the things for their peace. And, in contrast to modernity, their tradition held that the essential was a reality of a trans-human order. The Tao that might give them full humanity was not a matter of human creation or contrivance. It did not come into being when people talked and it did not slide into nothingness when people ceased talking. It was prior and human culture was secondary. It was obvious and human culture was dubious. When culture turned unreal, crazy, it continued as it had been. When culture hit a high point, knew a phase of health, it came clearly into focus. So any intelligent person made it the great treasure. Any master worth hearing gave it center stage.

22/47: SINGULARITY

"I alone am inactive and reveal no signs, like a baby that has not yet learned to smile. Listless as though with no home to go back to. The multitude have more than enough. I alone seem to be in want."

Rather remarkably, Lao Tzu here breaks out of his customary objectivity and injects a personal note. Probably he is characterizing any sage, not just himself, but still his own pains seep through. He alone is not busy about many things, making a stir in the everyday world. He alone seems driven into quietude, waiting for the Tao to reveal itself. This quietude keeps him from revealing himself. He has no heart for the business of self-promotion, the giving and receiving of confidences, that constitutes mercantile affairs, home life, a day at the government office. Those things have no appeal, perhaps even turn his stomach. He wants—he knows not what. He is sick at heart because his wanting has no definite object, cannot be laid out as a campaign he might win or lose. If he wanted a definite job, he could apply and take his chances. If he wanted a definite woman, he could woo her and let the chips fall. But since he wants the whole, the simple all, he suffers unmanageable fits of lassitude. These would be painful yet expectable in an adolescent. In a mature person they bespeak the contemplative crisis.

The contemplative crisis is the psychological manifestation of a theological truism: divinity is not a thing. The Tao or God is not an entity one can get one's hands on. It is not even an entity one can get one's mind around. It transcends particularity, definiteness, specific identity. We can be sure that it is, but we can never know what it is. And when our surety that it is goes into hiding, like the sun going behind the clouds, we can experience the finite world as a terrible, mocking game. Maybe there is no ultimate meaning. Maybe it is just flux and nonsense, Shakespeare's tale told by an idiot. In the horror that this might be, the mystics suffer the dark night of the soul. If they do their suffering in the East, they mainly have the pain of sensing the cracks in being. If they do their suffering in the West, they have the further burden of feeling sinful to the core and without chance for a redeemer.

This is a speculative interpretation of what Master Lao is saying, of course, and we cannot offer any surety that he meant all that we have read in. But we can be confident that the mystical experience, East and West, has similar patterns, and it is not hard to show that whenever people place their chips on the primacy of divinity they start a game of deep purification. Less interior personalities suffer analogous purifications, through what they learn in family life, the world of work, and the pains of their aging body. But the contemplative tends to suffer more globally and directly. The dark night of the senses is the need to have one's feelings reset by the truth that God is not a thing. The dark night of the soul is the desolation and repulsiveness one feels at being so far from God, morally even more than ontologically. And while either night holds sway, one still has to keep the fair side out, do one's bit in the world of public affairs, stifle the voice that wants to cry out that the whole chattery mess of commonplaces, banalities, mindless routines is a fraud driving one crazy.

The baby that has not yet learned to smile is very young. Neonatal studies have advanced since Lao Tzu's day, so we now know that from birth (if not in the womb) infants are striving to communicate. Nature has coded them to solicit responses, even to teach their bewildered parents how to give them attention, to stimulate their fresh learning systems that are revved up and ready to take off. When babies do not get this attention, cannot engage their parents, they grow sad and fail to thrive. Their little psyches are depressed by rejection and they can languish physically. But Lao Tzu probably has no such full scenario in mind. Probably he simply has seized the analogy of human being at its earliest, its least formed. As such it would be the uncarved block in spades. He has returned to the utmost simplicity, the purest potentiality, he can imagine. By losing himself in the Tao he has seemed to regress, to lose all the sophistication, the cleverness, the accomplishment society had prized. So he feels alone, abandoned, singular. The remarkable tone of these lines is the loneliness they convey. They come from a spirit paying a great price for its singular achievements. They remind us that when we go apart from the crowd we sacrifice warmth, familiarity, security. True, these have proven false gods, and while in their midst we used to feel suffocated. But we should not delude ourselves that striking out on our own will be all liberation, all joyous with relief and new vistas. No, it will carry an expensive price. We will sometimes wonder whether it isn't an inhuman adventure, something robbing us of friendship and acceptance.

So Lao Tzu feels listless—the Tao has withdrawn and he has burned his bridges back to the unreflective life. He feels he has no home. In the future the whole world may be his oyster but now, in this time of purification, he is an orphan, an alien. Twenty-three centuries before the existentialist literature of the 1950s Lao Tzu was speaking about alienation and estrangement. Yet his speech seems more authentic than what Heidegger, Sartre, and Camus were producing, because his gamble on the Tao was clearer than their gamble on—what? Their own spiritual rectitude? The best conscience one could develop in a godless, meaningless world?

The multitude have more than enough stimuli, intimations of possible meaning. They have small appetites for metaphysics, few needs for ontological assurance. If they can eat, drink, and be merry, they are satisfied. On his own terms, as we have indicated them in prior sections, Lao Tzu cannot condemn such people. They are living close to the earth. If they would only strip away the ersatz aspects of their ordinary lives, their equivalents of fast foods and obsession with the Stock Market, they might be admirably simple. On the other hand, to date their simplicity has not brought them to feel the Great Clod with unshod feet, to sense the stars pitching with the roll of the earth, to wonder about the silence of the heavens that swells at midnight, breaks out in the new baby's squall, seems still-born in the dead person's rictus. They have not been chilled and thrilled by the blast of cold air in that deep, quiet night. They have not felt the challenge to rise up on the breeze and travel to the farthest stars in pursuit of how it all fits together.

The sage wants to know how it all fits together. For the peace of his own soul, but also the peace of his country, he wants to know heaven's purposes for all the times he must endure. Soon he will go into the earth. He wants to be able to accept this as simple justice. But to do so he has to have sensed what has been going on, what human beings were supposed to have been doing, making, involved in. He's been put on a stage without having been furnished the script. He's been speaking, gesticulating, emoting without knowing how the scene's supposed to go. So he wants nothing and everything. He doesn't really care whether the scene is set in Beijing or Shanghai, he just wants to know there is a script, someone has written it, there will be a denouement.

For such a person, the alienations, the ignorances, the disorders that spawn our wars and social sufferings are a cosmic matter. We are as bellicose and unjust as we are because our whole interaction is tilted, corroded, diseased. Lacking roots in the Tao, our social relations are bound to wither and rot. Lacking ventilation to high heaven, they are bound to be dark and suffocating. Society itself has to pass through mystical purgations, if we are ever to dream of right living. Society itself has to be challenged, feel helpless as a new born, go through the lassitudes and depressions. Because there are few signs most people want to take on the mystical journey, there are few reasons for a Lao Tzu to expect the millennium. Because he himself has found the journey to be life-giving, to have made all the difference, to have shown him right order, he has to continue to hope.

Discussion Questions

1. Why has Chinese culture tended to think of Lao Tzu as suitable for retirement?
2. How do the classical symbols for the Tao challenge workaday assumptions about natural power?
3. What does "contending" call to the Taoist's mind?
4. How could *wu-wei* ever be an effective political style?
5. Why does the Taoist sage proceed through life like one fording a stream in winter?
6. Why should Taoist wisdom make the spirit murky like muddy water?
7. How does talk about benevolence and filial piety indicate decline from primal morality?
8. How fair is Lao Tzu's critique of the Confucians?
9. What does the uncarved block suggest would be the way to justice?

10. Why does mystical peace involve the loss of self-concern?

11. Why does Lao Tzu have to suffer alienation and abandonment?

12. What are the social analogues to the mystic's dark nights—the purifications the nations would have to go through to gain heavenly order?

Notes

1. See Thomas Merton, *The Way of Chuang Tzu* (New York: New Directions, 1968). On Taoism generally see Farzeen Baldrian *et al.,* "Taoism," ER, vol. 14, pp. 288–332; "Taoism," *Encyclopedia Britannica,* vol. 28 (Chicago: Encyclopedia Britannica, 1987), pp. 394–407; Holmes Welch, *Taoism: The Parting of the Way* (Boston: Beacon, 1966); H.G. Creel, *What is Taoism?* (Chicago: University of Chicago Press, 1970); Arthur Waley, *The Way and its Power* (New York, Grove Press, 1958); Chang Chung-yuan, *Creativity and Taoism* (New York: Harper Colophon, 1970); Wing-tsit Chan, *The Way of Lao Tzu* (Indianapolis: Bobbs-Merrill, 1963).

2. All translations are from D.C. Lau, *Lao Tzu: Tao Te Ching* (New York: Penguin, 1963). Lau thinks verse 21 is an interpolation.

3. For a Christian parallel, see Rosemary Haughton, *The Re-creation of Eve* (Springfield, Ill.: Templegate, 1985), pp. 22–24.

4. Modern political philosophers such as Rousseau also sensed that human nature needed to be redone. See Allan Bloom, *The Closing of the American Mind* (New York: Simon and Schuster, 1987), p. 189 (commenting on Rousseau's *The Social Contract,* II, 7).

121

Chapter 6

JUDAISM AND THE TALMUD

THE JEWISH WORLDVIEW

The last two traditions we treat, Judaism and Islam, bring us back into the Western orbit (although both may be considered Near-Eastern religions). Judaism, Christianity, and Islam are kindred traditions, despite their various antagonisms. All are prophetic, in contrast to the sapiential cast of Hinduism, Buddhism, and the Chinese traditions. All are monotheistic, take a linear view of history, reject reincarnation, think positively about material creation, look forward to a divine judgment on history, and lay great stress on social justice.

Judaism is the parent tradition, the mother often distressed to see what her offspring have become. This is clearer in the rise of Christianity as a Jewish sect than in the origin of Islam, but even those who stress the creativity of the revelations to Muhammad admit that Jewish and Christian ideas were available in sixth century C.E. Arabia. Most sketches of Jewish history name Abraham and Sarah as the place to begin, although they confess that it is hard to know how historical Abraham and Sarah were. Nonetheless, the traditions we have in Genesis about the ancestors seem likely to have had some basis in tribal memories. 1800 B.C.E. is a fair guess about the date of Abraham and Sarah.

To mention Genesis is to remind ourselves that the origins of Judaism are scriptural. The Bible is the main source Jews have used when thinking about their beginnings, and the Bible is perhaps best described as "paradigmatic" history. Without denying that such events as the revelations to Abra-

122

ham, the Exodus from Egypt, the giving of the Torah (Law) on Sinai through Moses, the kingdom of David and Solomon, and the Exile to Babylon actually happened, it is clear that the details interested the biblical compilers less than the lessons they offered later generations. If the Torah (first five books of the Bible) only came into loosely canonical form around 400 B.C.E., and the whole Hebrew Bible only reached something close to its present shape toward the end of the first century C.E., there were hundreds of years for priests, prophets, members of wisdom circles, and others to rework Israel's traditions so that their contemporary significance might shine the clearer. Thus Abraham, Moses, and David, along with Sarah, Miriam, and Bathsheba, became models, symbols, object lessons as much, probably even more, than historical personages.

The great events structuring the worldview of the Hebrew Bible were the Exodus, the Covenant, and the Exile. In light of the Exodus and the Covenant, Israel conceived the creation of the world as a preamble to the story of its own election. In light of the Exile later writers rethought the covenant, emphasizing that infidelity was bound to bring suffering. Throughout, the Exodus remained the greatest testimony to God's power and love. Throughout, the Torah given on Sinai framed Israel's understanding of what being bound to the Lord in covenant required of it. The kingship established with Saul and brought to a peak by David and Solomon made Zion polar to Sinai.[1] The worship in the Temple built by Solomon praised the Lord for having liberated Israel and established it in its own land even more than for his creation of the world. So the Bible has furnished Judaism a treasury of reflections on its bonds with its Lord. His having established the Mosaic covenant let Israel think it was unique among the nations on earth, possessed of a special relationship to God. Such central features of Jewish life as observing the Sabbath, keeping a kosher diet, circumcising newborn males, and studying Torah all stemmed from this sense of election.

After the Roman destruction of the Jerusalem temple in

70 C.E., the religious leaders of Israel established schools in the diaspora. They determined which holy writings would be considered authoritative, fashioning a whole from the Torah, historical and prophetic works, and miscellaneous writings. This whole, known as *Tanak* (an acronym from the first Hebrew letters for Torah-Prophets-Writings), had for several prior centuries informally furnished the rabbis their main matter for commentary. By around 200 C.E. such commentary, collected as the *Mishnah* ("Repetition"), was the major force in Jewish social life. The Mishnah itself generated commentary (known as the *Gemarah* ["Learning"]), and the combination of the Mishnah and the Gemarah about 500 C.E. produced the Talmud ("Study"). For the past fifteen hundred years religious Jews have considered the Talmud the best indication of the oral law tradition had long regarded as the complement to Tanak. Although Tanak, the Bible, had greater authority (traditional Judaism long held that Moses was the human author of Torah), the Talmud had great influence on practical matters such as how to keep the Sabbath, maintain a kosher kitchen, regulate marriages, bury the dead, transact business, and the like. And although talmudic scholarship varied somewhat according to geographic region (which region in turn determined under what alien religious rule Jews were living—Roman, Christian, Muslim), essentially both oriental and Western Jews followed the same main lines.

The basic assumptions governing talmudic Judaism include the biblical convictions we have already enumerated. There was but one God, who rendered all the gods of the nations idolatrous. This God had established a special relationship, the covenant, with the Jews. The world created by God was thoroughly good, which implied that fundamental human acts such as eating, drinking, having sexual relations, farming, studying, carrying out business, and praying all were honorable. Most honorable for pious Jews were praying and studying, but talmudic Judaism also thought that marrying and helping other people also were blessed by God.

This trinity of Jewish treasures—Torah, marriage, and good deeds—shaped the community life of Eastern European Jewry through its more than thousand year medieval period.[2] Torah implied studying, both to learn what God wanted in all details of daily life and to commune with the Lord, make one's own the thought-world of revelation. Study sometimes was forbidden to women, sometimes was not, but virtually always was a male preserve. Only men could be rabbis, could constitute the quorum of ten (*minyan*) necessary for prayer, and stood in the family as the representative of the Lord. Marriage was the common expectation, since Judaism sponsored no monastic life or celibate clergy. The great blessing of marriage was children, who helped parents fulfill the commandment to be fruitful and multiply and assured the chosen people another generation in which to praise its God. The good deeds that all Jews were to perform included helping the poor, caring for the sick, taking in the widow, the orphan, the wayfarer.

Through its regime of Torah, marriage, and good deeds, the Jewish community sought to be holy as befit the people the holy God had chosen for himself. Israel would be God's people, and he would be their Lord. The rules elaborated by the rabbis aimed at defining such holiness—making it practicable. So, for example, determining precisely when the Sabbath began and ended was a help to keeping the Sabbath fully. Making precise what animals were unclean and specifying the use of separate dishes was a help to cleanness, fittingness, holiness (various connotations of *kosher*) in the family's eating. Specifying hats for men, wigs for women, earlocks of hair for men—all such customs have helped pious Jews make concrete for themselves what holiness entailed. The same with women's visiting the ritual bath after menstruation, with men's praying in shawl and phylacteries, with the traditions about how to copy the Torah scrolls, with the laws about the marriage contract. The point to talmudic legislation was to help people know how to please God. From as far back as the legal sections of the Bible (for example, in Deuteronomy and

Leviticus), through the time of the Pharisees, Jewish teachers had pursued this goal. The talmudic rabbis merely sought to bring their predecessors' efforts up to date.

SHAB. 156B/221: CHARITY

"[R. Akiba] went forth and preached, 'Charity doth deliver from death—not merely from unnatural death but from death itself.' "[3]

Rabbi Akiba was the father of talmudic Judaism, the one most responsible for the work in the diaspora that gave birth to the Mishnah. The full story behind this saying tells us that he had a daughter whom the astrologers predicted would be bitten by a snake and so die on her wedding day. This worried the rabbi very much, but on her wedding day the daughter took her brooch and stuck it in the wall. Accidentally, it pierced the eye of a snake. The rabbi learned of this fact and asked his daughter for the details. She supplied as background the fact that the evening before a poor man had come to the door begging. Because everyone else was busy with the wedding preparations, she had given him the marriage gift her father had presented her. This struck R. Akiba as a great deed, and the more he thought about it the more he was convinced it had been the reason for her good fortune with the snake. Thus he uttered the lines quoted above.

The main point of the story, of course, is the splendor of charity. Those who are generous to the poor will greatly please Heaven. Whether the rabbi's words imply that charity brings resurrection is debatable, but they may, because by his time Judaism had developed the concept of resurrection to heavenly life. At any rate, certainly they imply that God cares for those who care for their fellow human beings, and certainly they also imply that charity builds up the life of the soul, countering the sinful tendencies that threaten it.

Both Judaism and Islam have tended to think about charity quite practically. It has brought to mind giving alms, offering people food, clothing, shelter, help with any worldly troubles. Judaism has not thought, as Buddhism has, about karma and detachment. Its first instinct has not been to purify the spirit, although certainly it has sponsored deep prayer and study. One did a good deed teaching others Torah. Love of neighbor certainly included concern and helpfulness regarding the neighbor's spiritual well-being. But more typical of what "charity" brought to mind was the act of Akiba's daughter. She saw a person in need and without hesitating gave of her own substance to help that person.

In the background of such a praiseworthy act stands the Jewish understanding of material creation. The goods of the earth come from God, and God always remains their first owner. This is perhaps clearest in the discussion of the Jubilee in Leviticus 25. It is because the land belongs to the Lord that it is to rest every seventh year and be returned to those who originally possessed it every fiftieth year. Similarly, it is because God is the source of all wealth and prosperity that people have an obligation to share them. When they share them generously, beyond what would be strictly necessary, as Akiba's daughter did, they pass from justice to charity. But doing good to others, helping them out, ought not to be considered exceptional. It ought to be considered a normal expression of the solidarity, the interrelatedness all human beings possess as made by one God.

The Jewish sense of charity undercut many arguments about justice and fair-dealing. Justice indeed was a central concern of Jewish ethics, but the rabbis were well aware that legal rectitude, simply helping or paying as the letter of the contract required, would never make the ideal community life. The ideal community life required people who were generous and went out of their way to do something extra. It was exemplified by the people honored in the synagogue as especially generous patrons. It was lively in the neighborhood through the good works of the women who looked out for the elderly, gave their extra clothes to the less fortunate, made sure that all the children had warm boots in winter.

The Buddhist virtue of compassion covers some of this ground, but without the warmth and personal involvement that Jewish charity suggests. Certainly, people could cross the line between charity and nosiness. Certainly, sometimes the village or the ghetto seemed to leave no place for privacy. But on the whole a sense of responsibility, involvement, and kindheartedness shaped Jewish ethics to a remarkable social awareness. On the whole Jewish charity made a good case for the positive possibilities in desire—in wanting everyone to flourish and enjoy life.

In Jewish perspective, life is something people should enjoy. God did make it good, beautiful, satisfying. So poverty has not been admirable in Jewish eyes, although certainly those who were poor through no fault of their own ought not to have been looked down upon by the Jewish community. Neither has asceticism been much admired, although moderation certainly has. When hard times have come, Jews have thought they should band even closer together, to share their resources and try to alleviate the pains of those suffering worst. Such times have borne out the wisdom of their tradition of charity, making the sharing of even last resources more possible than otherwise it would have been.

For our purposes, this last ingredient is probably the thing to stress. Charity—generosity, active compassion, habitual helpfulness—is not just the frosting on good times but the habitual attitude we need if we are to get through bad times with any grace. Of course charity frequently will be challenged. Whenever people do not act charitably in return, whenever they are hurtful, even hateful, we shall wonder whether trying to love other people and be helpful doesn't make us suckers. So the religious traditions have tried to root the key virtues—faith, hope, charity, compassion—in the very foundations of the divinity and its purposes for human beings.

In the Jewish case, charity has been a foundation of the entire covenant, in that the God who gave the covenant ultimately has been less a lawgiver intent on strict justice than a Lord compassionate and merciful, slow to anger and abounding in steadfast love.

When one meditated on this Lord—read the scriptures, studied the talmudic texts, prayed the daily and sabbath prayers—one was bound to be nurtured in sentiments deeper than most secular feelings about justice and peace. One was bound to emerge grateful for the largess of God and so inclined to show a similar largess to one's fellow human beings. The God who made the covenant got nothing of equivalent value in return. It was not because Israel had been the greatest of nations that the Lord had chosen it. It was solely because of God's own goodness, God's own unfathomable love. True, some passages of scripture describe God as jealous and bent on punishing sinners. But the deeper passages, the passages that come closest to the wonder and appreciation election and creation ought to generate, reveal God to move only because of God's own goodness. If God set out to be strictly just with human beings, who could survive? If God were always sensitive to God's rights and dignity, where would God's people be? No, God had shown divinity to be remarkably patient, long-suffering, willing to endure human follies and evils. Therefore, the images of God, the women and men covenanted to God, ought to think of charity as something habitual.

Were the nations to make charity something habitual, many of the world's claims of injustice and ventures into war would be undercut at a stroke. But we have contrived as social bodies to make charity something private, something we ought to consider unrealistic on a national or international scale. The people representing the nations are more likely to have been trained as lawyers than as rabbis. They are more likely to be interested in advancing the prosperity of their constituents than in helping others less fortunate. Certainly there are technical reasons why the wealthy nations keep getting wealthier and the poor nations keep getting poorer, but there are also reasons lodged in people's hearts. Were there more charity, more instinctive conviction that God delights in our helping the poor, there could be much less poverty and suffering.

TAAN. 20B/229: FORGIVENESS

"A man should always be soft as a reed and not hard like a cedar."

If charity offers us one way to undercut movements toward war and grievances about injustice, forgiveness offers us another. For the rabbis such forgiveness was a two-way street. People who suspected they had given offense were to ask forgiveness. People who had been offended were to grant forgiveness. To buttress this attitude, the rabbis counseled that when one had done someone a slight wrong one ought to consider it a major injury. In other words, the best way to nip estrangement in the bud was to consider any offensive action of one's own significant. On the other hand, when one had been offended the best attitude was to minimize the offense. Relatedly, those who did good deeds were wise to consider them nothing much, small benefits, while those who received even small benefactions were wise to consider them great gifts. In this way, mutual help and respect might thrive, while taking offense, being hurt and angered, might lessen.

Forgiveness was also a way to undercut vengeance. In one homey example, a person who asks to borrow his neighbor's sickle is refused. The next day, the neighbor comes by to borrow an axe. If the one who owns the axe refuses to lend it, because he is still smarting from having been denied the sickle, he will be exacting revenge and so further worsening relations with his neighbor. If he forgets the neighbor's previous boorishness and lends him the axe, he certainly will avoid the corrosive force of vengeance in his own soul and he may set relations back on the right track. Further, he may give his neighbor such good example that the neighbor will reconsider his prior boorishness and himself become cooperative.

Forgiveness is the tape with which one can repair slashed social relations. It is the antidote that can counteract the poisons of injustice and hate. And, like charity, it breaks us out of the circle of strict justice, wherein social life is likely to suffocate. Strict justice, in the sense of hurt and punishment (counter-hurt), is endless. It does little to repair damage from the past and works more destruction. Even when punishment is measured, punishment alone is unlikely to persuade wrongdoers, either criminals or good people who just lashed out in a fit of anger or frustration, that people can do better than the law of the talon, the mentality of an eye for an eye and a tooth for a tooth.

In the theology of the Hebrew Bible, two views of the covenant fought for supremacy. The first, most evident in the book of Deuteronomy and the Deuteronomistic history (Joshua through Kings), postulated that if Israel kept the codes of the covenant it would prosper and if it broke them it would feel punishment. Both the prosperity and the punishment would be quite physical: wealth flowing into the kingdom, wine and parties everywhere; pain flowing into the kingdom, foreign soldiers putting their boots on people's necks. The imagery behind this first view of the covenant was economic and legalistic. God would have to repay Israel as befit its fidelity or infidelity, because the covenant was a *quid pro quo,* a balance of payments in and payments out. In the name of his own justice, God would have to punish those who had dishonored his name, had forgotten his benefactions and repudiated his love. So, to the theologians who espoused this first view of the covenant, it made sense that after Solomon the kingdom fell apart, and that as the kings of the divided realm continued to do evil in the sight of the Lord both half-kingdoms would suffer political decline, culminating in the fall of the North to Assyria and the fall of the South to Babylon.

The second view of the covenant, which we see emerging in the major prophets and culminating in Second Isaiah (chapters 40–55), sensed that the God who had chosen Israel out of love would be moved to succor her in her sufferings, to free her from Exile and restore her to the promised land. This God would not be bound by an economic, legalistic view of the compact between himself and Israel but would treat her as his bride, his child, one he loved irrationally. In a change of figures, the prophets sensed that God would be like a nursing mother, unable to abandon her child. God would be moved to the womb with feelings of regret and compassion at the sufferings entailed in the Exile.[4] In other words, the divine love would find a way to forgiveness and restoration. The divine goodness would not let itself be imprisoned by Israel's wrongdoing but would be creative enough to love Israel out of its sinfulness.

Ultimately, therefore, the talmudic call to forgiveness and new beginnings could claim to be moving in tracks the Lord himself had laid down. It was not accidental that the prophets also called Israel to stress mercy rather than sacrifice, to let justice roll down like a mighty stream. When tempted to wars of vengeance, the people ought to think about beating their swords into plowshares. When irritated with one another, they ought to heed God's invitation and sit down to reason together. Thus the Word of God, which the prophets claimed to announce, offered Israel a context much wider than ordinary justice. Because divinity itself, the creative mystery responsible for the world and the great liberator who had led the people out of Egypt, had displayed tolerance, forgiveness, generosity, the people covenanted to him ought to know better than to box themselves into a framework of tit for tat.

East and West, divinity has served justice not only by seconding the voices of conscience that tell us what is right and wrong, fair and unfair, but also by keeping justice in perspective. From a heavenly point of view, human beings have few rights before God. Job, despite all the impressive evidence he can produce that he has done no wrong and is suffering unfairly, has no answer when God speaks out of the whirlwind and asks him if he knows the measure of the universe.[5] True, God supports Job against his "friends" who keep accusing him, but God never lets Job think human perceptions of justice are the last word. In the realm of creation, we come from nothingness and only stay in being through God's on-going grant of existence. In the realm of salvation, where God heals our brokenness, everything is grace. Such perspectives are a mighty inducement to back away from our all-too-human tendency to bristle when we have been offended, to be ever on the lookout for affronts to our dignity, abridgements of our rights. Many people know this personally, accept the relevance of religious perspectives when it comes to smoothing things in the family, around the neighborhood, on the job. But to date we have been hit or miss in translating religious wisdom into foreign policy, policy about our own poor, educational programs that might undercut the competitiveness and litigiousness complicating, often ruining, business and international affairs. Of course it is simplistic to claim that if people believed in a loving God or honored a compassionate Buddhnature they would quickly make everything right in political affairs. On the other hand, it is equally simplistic to divorce public policy from ultimate perspectives, to think about economics or diplomacy in the cramped horizon of this-worldly justice.

By and large, both professional politicians (statesmen, military personnel, governors) and intellectuals accept the first proposition: religious convictions about the primacy of the divine cannot be imported directly into political decision-making without grave risk. The second proposition (this-worldly justice is an inadequate perspective for solving major social problems) still awaits general approval. Practically, if not theoretically, most public officials are atheists or agnostics. Even if they want to gain a better horizon, they don't know how to integrate it with their tactics for advancing justice and peace. The Talmud won't immediately teach them how, but a little reading in the rabbis could do them a world of good. For then they might see why the soft reed is better than the hard wood. Then they might glimpse why forgiveness is not a luxury but a virtue the nations need every day.

SHAB. 31A/65: THE GOLDEN RULE

"What is hateful to yourself do not to your fellow-man. That is the whole of the Torah and the remainder is but commentary. Go, learn it."

This famous saying from R. Hillel occurs in a story meant to contrast Hillel and Shammai, his rival for rabbinical eminence in the first years of the Common Era. A heathen came to Shammai asking to be accepted as a convert to Judaism. However, he imposed one condition: Shammai was to teach him the whole of the Torah while he stood on one foot. Shammai threatened to clout him with a yard-stick, apparently thinking him a schlemiel. The man went to Hillel with the same request. Hillel's response is our text. In addition to offering an epitome of the Torah, it suggests Hillel's flexibility when it came to helping people grasp the Torah.

We have seen this golden rule in Confucius, and it occurs in the teachings of Jesus (perhaps drawing from Hillel), where it is in positive form: Do unto others as you would have them do unto you (Matthew 7:12). Hillel is bold enough to consider the golden rule the whole of God's instruction for Israel. To his mind, then, the Torah was meant to teach people mutual considerateness, thus enabling them to grasp what others wanted, needed, and render it as though fulfilling a want or need of one's own. All the minutiae of the laws were but commentary, gloss, elaboration. Grasp this core and the rest would follow easily enough.

A humanistic mind, wanting to tie religious teachings to what people actually experience and make it bear on their liberation from injustice, comes upon summaries, digests, of the Torah, the Gospel, the Qur'an, the Dharma as upon manna sent from heaven. As the Catholic theologian Karl Rahner emphasized again and again, the modern world has become far too complex for any individual to master. We all need short formulas of faith that show us the heart of the matter. If these form our consciences and lead us into the keeping of the Holy Spirit, we will have the inner touchstones we need to evaluate as best we can the manifold data pouring in. Thus the primacy of love has served many Christians as an epitome of the gospel. One of Rahner's own summaries was, "God gives himself." The Buddha's Four Noble Truths have served as a summary of the Middle Way. The Confucians, when pushed, have made it all a matter of *jen.* So Rabbi Hillel stands in good company. Like the Buddha, Jesus, and Confucius, he had much more to say, but when pushed he was able and willing to put it all in a nutshell. Blessings on such teachers.

What, then, has the rabbi told us? How ought his words to be taken? Insofar as the Torah has been the great treasure of Jewish life (prior to Hillel, in his day, and ever since), the rabbi has suggested that God's Instruction ought but to sensitize human beings and make them consider other people their radical equals. What one person hates, others are likely to hate as well. Therefore, the person who hates being lied to must take care himself never to lie. The person who cringes in fear and shame from a tongue-lashing by her boss must take care not to brow-beat her children. We can learn from what we hate, and love, what others find despicable and pleasing. Rabbi Hillel is sanguine about human solidarity. We are more alike than different. If any of us are cut we will bleed. If any of us are abused, beaten, despised, we will suffer, feel woefully diminished. Such solidarity is enough to sketch out both how

135

we ought to treat others and what criterion we ought to use in evaluating others' consistency.

On further examination, of course, we find that people not only share certain basic attitudes but also differ from one another in their likes, dislikes, reactions to praise, reactions to punishment. The rabbi's teaching is not the whole story. But it is the most important chapter, all the more so when one switches from a detached description of how people react to an involved, serious quest to know how we ourselves ought to act and react. We ought to assume that what we find hateful will strike others the same way. We ought to enter into other people's sufferings with the expectation that what is afflicting them would also afflict us.

Consider slavery, racism, sexism, religious prejudice. Each is a complicated issue, with historical, philosophical, psychological, sociological dimensions. Yet each also is a concept abstracted from millions of individual cases. Each also may be simplified in millions of cases to "something hateful." For action to reform our own behavior, or the behavior of our society at large, we need not know much more than this hatefulness. Certainly it helps to learn the history and psychology of racism or sexism. Certainly contributing to lessening either will involve educating those not yet able to feel the hatefulness in their bones, as something they too might suffer. But the first thing is letting oneself see and feel such hatefulness. The first thing is having an imagination opened by the Torah, a sensibility alive with *mit-sein:* awareness that existence is shared, communal, a matter of brother-and-sisterhood.

Where are we to go and learn these things? How does such a sensibility develop? We can study the scriptures for lessons, taking the prophets and the sages as models. We can concentrate on the *mahatmas:* the Buddha, Lao Tzu, Muhammad. But we must also look around us, inspect our own hearts, expect to find any living Torah or Gospel pertinent to where we work, worship, recreate. When we walk the beach, enjoying the water lapping at our feet, liking the rough rub of the sand, we should take a lesson from the disgust the candy wrappers and pop cans arouse. If others don't share this disgust enough not to litter, we should account them retarded and so pathetic, people deserving the help of our better example. When we walk the inner city streets, skirting the common, we should take a lesson from the reaction the drunks and panhandlers arouse. At first the lesson may seem to be that we shouldn't bother other people, as these derelicts are bothering us. On reflection we may realize we would hate to be in the position of having to beg from other people, would feel angry and ashamed, so probably they are feeling that way, hoping we don't further diminish them.

How do we feel when the textbooks of another country portray our society as centered on drugs and crime? What corrections does such a feeling suggest about our depictions of other societies? How do we feel when the Stock Market crashes and our financial security is threatened? What does this suggest about the emotions of people brought low by unemployment, about countries regularly depressed, about poverty as sucking away life's joy?

Such a technique is all too hazy and all too relevant. It can seem to manufacture platitudes, yet each of them is a window onto the self, the human condition. Once we authors were in a foreign country, trying to get news about a job back home that we desperately wanted. After waiting hours to arrange the trans-oceanic call (to a person who ought to have gotten word to us by mail weeks before), we finally got through—only to have him refuse to accept the call, because the time wasn't convenient. That experience has stayed with us as a testimony not only to one person's lack of imagination and so humanity but also to the obtuseness responsible for so much unnecessary pain. Parents who don't work hard to remember what adolescence was like, men who never try to imagine what being a woman entails, adults who have no patience with old people, the well-to-do who write the poor off as simply lazy, clerics who don't try to learn about family life, subordinates who never think about the burdens of leadership—all give much pain because they don't try to imagine, haven't got the basic *sympatico* Hillel and others think goes with human skin. We cannot give other people new psyches, but we can try to discipline our own psyches to the golden rule.

TAAN. 22A/204: PEACEMAKING

> "A Rabbi was standing in the market place when Elijah appeared to him. The Rabbi asked him, 'Is there anybody in this market-place who will have a share in the World to Come?' Elijah answered there was not. In the meantime there came two men and Elijah said, 'These will have a share in the World to Come.' The Rabbi asked them, 'What is your occupation?' They answered, 'We are merrymakers; when we see men troubled in mind we cheer them up, and when we see two men quarreling we make peace between them.' "

We might note, first, that once again we are dealing with a story. The rabbis, developing biblical tradition, regularly did business by telling stories. Abstract principles might elucidate the intellectual crux of a matter, what the mind had found when bent to analysis, but only a story could give such principles flesh and blood. Second, we might note that the rabbi is eager to learn. Providentially brought into contact with Elijah, the greatest of the non-writing prophets (and a figure associated with the coming of the Messiah), his first instinct is to profit, to learn.

Third, what is it the rabbi wants to learn? Something about the world to come: heaven, fulfillment, permanent blessing from God. Looking around the market place, the rabbi decides to use it to learn from Elijah what is requisite for salvation. Here is a group of ordinary people. What distinguishes those pleasing to God from those who will not receive God's best blessing? We don't learn why Elijah rejects the whole group as unworthy of the world to come. Perhaps the story intends a rigorist warning: the path is narrow and those who stay on it are few. Perhaps the implication is that simple decency, gracing the market place with honest enough desires and causing no trouble, is not enough.

Fourth, the two men who get Elijah's approval, who have the right stuff, apparently show the rabbi nothing impressive. He has to ask what they do, how they make their way in this world, before he gets an inkling of their virtue. And what he learns is delightful, cheering indeed: they are clowns, comedians, entertainers. They take people's minds off their worries and bring them laughter, distraction, the perspective that irony, satire, and the mismatch of person and role can bring. As well, they are peacemakers, ever alert to throw water on the fires of dispute, ever trying to reconcile neighbor to neighbor.

Let us reflect on both of the men's functions. First, that they are merrymakers reminds us of the humor in the Hebrew Bible. One of the main differences between the Old and the New Testament is the fun the authors of the Old Testament have. The New Testament, dominated by the passion and death of Jesus, is too gripped by tragedy to have the psychic freedom to play with human folly. The Old Testament, dealing with long-past legends and compiled as something of a grab-bag, a collection of whatever different Israelite schools found useful, has more distance, more detachment. So again and again we find it trading in ironies: Jacob, the wily one, is out-wilied by Laban. Elijah, at war with the priests of Baal, asks them whether their deity has gone aside to relieve himself. Sarah laughs at the deity's promise that in her old age she will bear a child—little chance of that, she reckons bawdily. And so it goes. Even when the prophets are in high dudgeon they can tee off on Israel with biting humor.

Here, however, the humor seems gentler. The merrymakers want to take away troubles. They want to create the equivalent of a snug bar, with a warm fire and a jar of poteen. If music calms our savageness, humor makes us forget our burdens and pains. How? In good part by taking us outside ourselves. The more we narrow in on our money troubles, our family tensions, our dissatisfactions at work, the stupidity of our elected leaders, the more depressed we become. We have forgotten past history, which was just as full of knaves and fools. We have forgotten vast nature, which pays our follies little mind. And we have forgotten God, who can turn our tragedies, petty or great, into comedy. From God's perspective, we are all simpletons, bumblers, people far too inclined to take ourselves seriously. The grass withers, the flowers fade, but the Word of the Lord endures forever. Surely the people, ourselves, are but grass.

Blessed, then, are the merrymakers, who lighten our hearts and prepare us to be religious: grateful to God for the basic graces—our health, our children, the light of our eyes and the air we breathe. Blessed, as well, are the peacemakers, and how interesting that the same two men are both merrymakers and peacemakers. Indeed, which of these two occupations is more crucial to their being fit for the Kingdom of Heaven? Will they be in the world to come because they have caused people to laugh or because they have kept them from one another's throats? Or are these misguided questions? Is the point rather the proximity of merrymaking and peacemaking?

Let us suppose that it is. In that case, the work of God would proceed by laughter and pacifying. It would take people out of their narrowed perspectives and join them to one another in better cheer. Probably it would use that better cheer to jolly them into cooling their irritations with one another. Probably it would make all parties to a potential blowup feel a little foolish, a little sheepish. Instinctively, most peoples have used the tribal campfire, the neighborhood pub, the monthly family gathering to kindle good feelings, belly-laughs, and the easing of tensions. When possible they have stayed far from potentially murderous tensions by letting the cut-ups ply their trade, the women do their soothing. Once again, the problem is to translate these ancient strategies for new global situations where the groups are vast and the tensions have escalated.

Recently, we have seen significant politicians get by largely on good humor, bonhommie. Like the last of Salome's seven veils, their balminess has hidden their emptiness. Yet we have been so grateful for the distraction and call to laughter that we have forgiven them too many sins. We have lowered merrymaking from a godly art to a something shameful, a fugue from responsibility. Thus merry-making, like the golden rule, proves on analysis to be complicated. When the wisdom literature wants to paint a contrast to the sage, it speaks of the fool—the person so superficial he or she giggles away the night and day. The story about the rabbi meeting Elijah therefore probably assumes that life is serious, people usually are straining to survive and follow the commands of their Lord. The merrymakers/peacemakers come onto a stage cast in such shadows. They are vehicles of grace because they suggest how God's touch, the stirring of the Spirit, immediately brings light and joy.

One might take this hypothesis in several directions, but the one that occurs to us now is celebration. Religious groups regularly develop celebratory rituals. Sometimes, as with the ritual for the Day of Atonement, Yom Kippur, they are grim and mournful. Sometimes, as with the ritual for Purim, they are light and frothy. But always they intend to bring people before a God whose final word is yes, whose final emotion is love, who wants the life of the sinner rather than the sinner's destruction. And perhaps the most touching of the rituals one finds across the span of the world's religions is the sanctified meal. It takes food and drink and makes them sacraments. Building on the relaxation and trust natural to table fellowship, it uses the family meal to suggest the ideal community, what fellowship will be like in the world to come. Thus when it waxed messianic Judaism spoke of the messianic banquet—the great party the coming of God's anointed would usher in. When it celebrated the Sabbath it put out the best linen, the best silver, and bid people be openhanded, invite in the wayfarer, enjoy. Blessed, in such circumstances, were the merrymakers, for they found it easy to be peacemakers. Blessed were the wits, the people able to mock their own pretensions, those who made everyone laugh at human folly, those who moved everyone away from vindictiveness, hatred, and violence.

SIFRE DEUT. 16 (68B)/209: JUSTICE

"If the Gentile comes to be judged by the Jewish code, then decide accordingly; if he wishes to be judged by the Gentile code, then decide accordingly."

Our text is the opinion of R. Simeon b. Gamaliel, the son of a famous Pharisee. He was opposing the opinion of R. Ishmael, who had urged rabbis to use whatever code, Jewish or Gentile, gave the best chance of favoring the suit of the Jewish party. R. Simeon, R. Akiba, and others denounced this favoritism. Even though Jews frequently could not get justice when dealing with Gentile authorities, most rabbis refused to let their own administration of justice be compromised. Their Lord wanted evenhandedness whether judges were dealing with the rich or the poor, with Jews or Gentiles. Justice was an attribute of divinity itself, not to the exclusion of mercy but as a consequence of the divine truth. Thus it lay on all Jews as a task, a work of imitation. Rabbis charged with deciding lawsuits therefore were counseled to bend over backwards not to be influenced contrary to the facts of the case. Indeed, one rabbi disqualified himself when he found that the man who had helped him across a bridge would be coming before him as a plaintiff.

The Bible is explicit in prohibiting the taking of bribes (Exodus 23:8). The Talmud added that this prohibition extended to bribes that might acquit the innocent or condemn the guilty (Keth. 105a). And "bribe" came to stand for more than a payment of money. It came to stand for anything that might prejudice the verdict, anything that might keep the judge from hearing, seeing, following the whole truth. To the talmudic mind, the influence-peddling rampant in our society probably would seem systematic bribery. Our lobbyists, deal-makers, middlemen all seek not the elaboration of truth before an impartial judge but to soften the judge (decision-maker, one who will decide how the law is written or who gets the contract) up. To be sure, some of such activity can be defended as the price a democratic system pays for making the political process a free-for-all in which all have the right to speak up, make their case. But the judges certainly still have to walk carefully and keep their consciences clean, and the whole process would benefit greatly from everyone's recalling that the common good often suffers from wheeling and dealing.

The talmudic world saw the evils of wheeling and dealing more clearly than we do because it had a deeper sense of people's needs, both as individuals and in community. The world to come impinged on talmudic judges. They had to consider both their own integrity, as that would be questioned by God, and the heavenly welfare of the people standing before them. This did not have to make them rigorists, ideologues bound to downplay the material aspects of a case in favor of safeguarding spiritual ideals. But it did imply an anthropology different from that of the philosophers (Locke, Jefferson, Madison) who shaped our American sense of the common good.

In our culture, the profit motive is quite accepted, even sanctified. As long as everyone has a chance to benefit, to play

143

in the game, we accept the principle of (more or less enlightened) self-interest. This goes along with our essentially utilitarian view of economics, politics, and human nature. What makes for wealth and satisfaction is good. What makes for want, pain, soul-searching is bad. The world to come is a nuisance, or at least an awkwardness, because it doesn't fit into a utilitarian calculus very well. To be sure, some theologians have tried to make heaven just another business venture, but that hasn't computed very successfully. No, the biblical symbols for heaven, God, divine judgment, and the rest have been stronger than our efforts to make them just the last chapter of our utilitarian story, the overtime of our democratic game. They have continued to imply that God's ways may not be our ways, that God's "profitable" may deal us heavy losses.

The point is that such symbols, as brooded over by the rabbis and correlated with biblical and talmudic law, kept the notion of justice cleaner than our utilitarian symbols have allowed. It gave justice some of the aura of the divine holiness. To take bribes or open oneself to the influence-peddlers was to desecrate the processes (imperfect, but nonetheless fraught with religious significance) by which God's people tried to establish fair-dealing. To pray over the laws of God and surrender oneself to the inscrutable divine justice was to remove oneself from the hurly-burly of slanted human influences, to open one's roof and let in a heavenly light.

This does not deny that American legal traditions also were hard on bribery, nor that they had their highminded views of justice. The figure of justice as a blindfolded woman with a scale preweighted on neither side expresses the somewhat rationalistic but nonetheless impressive American ideal. The problem is all the political, pragmatic, utilitarian factors that now impinge on our legal system, and even more on decisions in government. The problem is finding enough people in positions of responsibility, enough people who have to make important decisions, who still think of human nature in more than utilitarian terms. One is not likely to outrun utilitarianism unless one nourishes a streak of contemplation. One is not likely to go below the increasingly thin band of pragmatism unless one meditates and prays. Perhaps many of those charged with important decision-making do, but the impression one gets of how executives, politicians, and lawyers now tend to live is not reassuring.

For example, it is hard to imagine good decision-making when the decision-maker is working 80 hours a week, talking all day, eating on the run, always reading and writing against the clock. It is hard to imagine even-handed political representation and decision-making when politicians have to raise money for their campaigns, please their constituents back home, and always avoid the impression of having backed the wrong horse or lost in the political infighting. One may defend this system as the best a group of people originally representing many different religious and regional colonies could have come up with, but that should not blind us to the ways it fails the biblical ideals of justice. Enlightened self-interest and checks and balances for a human nature considered selfish from the outset are considerably less than highly disciplined openness to what under God seems fair.

This remains true even when we place the American system of justice in the perspective of the world's many systems and come away thinking it fares quite well. It remains true even when we agree that abuses of a system shouldn't be taken as flaws intrinsic to the system itself and when we admit that people in most times and places have not been saintly. The rabbinic ideal was not always realized. The very conflict between rabbis Simeon and Ishmael shows how the Jewish best and brightest had to fight for their ideals. Nonetheless, there breathes in the rabbinic texts a fineness of spirit, a delicacy of conscience, that doesn't appear very often in the annals of present-day American justice. Instead one gets the impression that the rabbis' ideals usually would be mocked as impractical, idealistic, out of touch with the base motives driving almost all players in almost all games. The difference is that the rabbis had not become cynical about either human nature or God's laws and grace. They still thought people thrived by being called to strict honesty, to pure conscience, to full freedom from base motives and bribery. Can this coexist with, even inform, a realistic, compassionate sense of what actually is possible among human beings? Can it bring heavenly standards down to earth, rather than creating more cynicism because such standards prove utopian? The rabbis thought it could, so they kept struggling mightily. It's not clear our principal authorities retain such faith. If one looks at what they do, how they let their game be played, rather than at what they say on the Fourth of July, one can be very discouraged. But that, in turn, can make one realize why scripture says we have here no lasting city. That, in turn, can help us render to Caesar what is Caesar's and keep from Caesar the large portion of our allegiance that is God's.

Discussion Questions

1. What sort of death does charity defeat?
2. Why wasn't R. Akiba distressed that his daughter had given away his wedding present to her?
3. Should forgiveness depend on the repentance of the one who has given offense?
4. What place is there for forgiveness in law and politics?
5. How valid is the psychological assumption of the golden rule that people share a similar sensibility about what is hateful?
6. How valid is the charge that the golden rule is humanistic pap incompatible with the particularistic (ethnic, religious) source of people's actual vitality and strong culture?
7. What is necessary to make "Let us eat, drink, and make merry" into a religious counsel?

8. How could merry-making segue into peace-making?

9. What sort of justice can one realistically expect from decision-makers in a pluralistic society?

10. Why is the Torah not utilitarian?

Notes

1. See Jon D. Levenson, *Sinai and Zion* (Minneapolis: Winston/Seabury, 1985). On Judaism in general, see Eugene M. Borowitz *et al.,* "Judaism," ER, vol. 8, pp. 127–204; *Encyclopedia Judaica,* 17 vols. (Jerusalem: Keter, 1972 ff.); *Back to the Sources,* ed. Barry W. Holtz (New York: Summit Books, 1984); Norman K. Gottwald, *The Hebrew Bible: A Socio-Literary Introduction* (Philadelphia: Fortress, 1985); *The Hebrew Bible and its Modern Interpreters,* ed. Douglas A. Knight and Gene M. Tucker (Philadelphia: Fortress, 1985); *The Torah: A Modern Commentary,* ed. W. Gunter Plaut (New York: Union of American Hebrew Congregations, 1981); *Take Judaism, For Example,* ed. Jacob Neusner (Chicago: University of Chicago Press, 1983).

2. See Mark Zborowski and Elizabeth Herzog, *Life is With People* (New York: Schocken, 1962).

3. All translations are from A. Cohen, *Everyman's Talmud* (New York: Schocken, 1975). For each text we give both the talmudic reference, according to the standard abbreviations, and the page in *Everyman's Talmud.*

4. On the maternity of God in the Hebrew Bible, see Phyllis Trible, *God and the Rhetoric of Sexuality* (Philadelphia: Fortress, 1978).

5. See Gustavo Gutierrez, *On Job* (Maryknoll, N.Y.: Orbis, 1987).

Chapter 7

ISLAM AND THE QUR'AN

THE MUSLIM WORLDVIEW

We have mentioned that Judaism, Christianity, and Islam share a family resemblance. Sometimes comparativists refer to these as Abrahamic religions, since all three honor Abraham as the father of their faith. Muslims themselves have considered Jews and Christians "People of the Book" (people formed by scriptures like the Qur'an) and so unlike ancient Greeks or Buddhists. Like Judaism and Christianity, Islam has had a powerful scripture that grounded a full legal tradition (*Shariah*). In addition to the Qur'an, the main authorities in Islamic life have been the traditions about the sayings and behavior of Muhammad (*hadith*), community consensus, and analogical reasoning. All four sources of authority have supported a strong conviction that Allah wants justice from human beings.

The revelations that transformed Muhammad (570–632 C.E.) from the manager of a caravan business to a world-shaping prophet stressed the coming of God in judgment. The Arabs to whom Muhammad preached were to repent of their idolatries and repair the cracks of injustice in their society. One might say that such idolatries had been depriving Allah of what Allah was owed, and that submitting fully to the one true God (becoming a devout Muslim) was the way to redress such injustice. Similarly, accepting the Muslim social code would mean assuming responsibility for the widows, the orphans, the poor who were slipping through the cracks of Arab society. Muhammad had been orphaned as a young child, and

148

he had married a (wealthy) widow, so he knew about those two vulnerable stations.

The trade that had made the Mecca of Muhammad's day prosperous was a danger to both sorts of justice. The pagan traditions of pre-Islamic Arabia begot a flourishing business in amulets, charms, and visits to the famous shrine (*Ka'ba*) nearby. The traditional clan system had broken down in the rush to profit from such trade, so Muhammad sought to reconstitute Arab society on the basis of a religious brother-and-sisterhood that would undercut clan loyalties and hostilities alike. Thenceforth, if one were languishing as a widow, orphan, or common poor person, one would have a claim on the alms all Muslims were to contribute toward the care of the unfortunate.

However, the greatest lesson of Muhammad's revelations (and so of the Qur'an that collected those revelations) was the surpassing grandeur of Allah. The revelations sought to strip the Arab psyche of its polytheism, rendering the oneness, the soleness of Allah like the sun presiding over the desert. Nothing could be compared with Allah. Allah shared divinity with nothing else (it was unthinkable that Allah should have a divine Son, like the Christian God). Nature had come from Allah as a series of testimonies to the divine grandeur. It was good in itself, and human beings were to be vice-gerents of Allah, ruling it justly for the prosperity of all. Allah had fashioned human beings from a clot of blood—lowly beginnings indeed. Their vocation was to submit to Allah like slaves to their benign master. Indeed, to obey Allah was the peak of human opportunity and achievement. For Allah alone held power, knew human beings' fate, deserved praise and thanksgiving.

The first of the five "pillars" popularly considered to summarize Islam condenses this theology into a memorable formula: There is no God but Allah, and Muhammad is his Prophet. Through Muhammad Allah has given human beings all that they require to serve him and pass the tests of Judgment Day. Muhammad seals, consummates, the line of prophecy begun with Abraham, forwarded by Moses and Jesus, but diverted in latter days. Such prior prophets deserve honor and respect, but Muhammad stands above them, unique and alone. He is the definitive mouthpiece of Allah, whose Qur'an ("Recital") will have no successor. Later Muslim theology speculated about the Qur'an much as Judaism had speculated about the Torah and Christianity had speculated about the Logos, making it the eternal companion of Allah. But on earth Muhammad was the fully authoritative medium of divine revelation, the one through whom the Qur'an gained human voice and whose life became the model of the perfect Muslim, the full submitter to Allah.

The other four pillars of Islam enjoined praying five times a day, fasting during the month of Ramadan, giving alms, and making the pilgrimage to Mecca. All four helped Muslims live out the first pillar as a common faith. Prayer traditionally has been made facing Mecca. Fasting has imposed a common discipline and been juxtaposed to the common partying that goes on during the nights of Ramadan (fasting is from the beginning of light to the end). The alms has reminded Muslims of their solidarity and given material form to their obligation to care for one another. The pilgrimage has taken Muslims back to their common center and entailed a common clothing and set of observances that leveled social distinctions.

Because Muhammad was convinced that the revelations come to him were an imperative of Allah, he endured the initial rejection of most of his fellow Meccans and continued to preach what Allah had disclosed to him (through the angel Gabriel). When tensions arose, he not only persevered in his preaching but seized the opportunity to make Medina, a city 320 kilometers from Mecca, a base from which he could finally defeat the recalcitrant Meccans in battle. From this start Islam has felt an imperative to spread Qur'anic revelation and has justified aggression against those who would have denied it free expression. *Jihad,* meaning holy resistance or war, has gained interior meanings (struggling against what hampers the religious soul), but it has retained the notion of resisting those who would deny Islam full flourishing.

Peace therefore has not sounded in Muslim ears the way it has sounded to Buddhists. Muslims did not approve slaughter and destruction, but they expected to fight for their faith and enjoined on all the responsibility of aiding those brought into conflict with outsiders because of the faith. Justice has included the notion that Allah has sovereign rights, default from which greatly lessens any human being's claim to gentle treatment. Islam has no tradition of separating secular and sacred matters and no tradition of constructing a pluralistic state in which all religious groups, and nonbelievers, would be equal under the civil law. Its traditional political thought assumes the rightness of theocracy as well as the supremacy of Muslims in any Islamic country.

As is true of pre-modern culture generally, Islam has made more of human beings' duties as members of the Muslim community (*ummah*) than of their rights as free or independent agents. Muslim women, like women in all of the other religious traditions we have treated, have not shared the opportunities for leadership open to men and have suffered from a misogynistic strain that considered them less than fully human. On the other hand, they have had rights guaranteed by the Qur'an and traditional Muslims (again like traditional interpreters of other religious worldviews) have used an argument of "separate but complementary" to indicate women's considerable dignity.

For the pious Muslim, the overriding reality has been the will and presence of Allah. Although Allah transcended the world, he was also as near as the pulse at one's throat. Similarly, although he was the Lord of the Worlds and would judge the worlds strictly, one recited the Qur'an "in the name of Allah, the Compassionate, the Merciful." Those who kept faith with him could expect to avoid the Fire and gain the Garden. Muslim mystics celebrated the presence of Allah in both creation and the soul. They sought union with him, in the process sometimes introducing a theme of love that softened the slave/master relation more officially approved. The Sufis became great story-tellers and ascetics bent on showing the path to Allah, the path that is straight. In their wisdom and fervor they balanced the lawyers and suggested that "justice" has a dimension of feeling which laws alone can neither express nor assure.[1]

49:8*/268: THE JUST

"If two parties of believers take up arms the one against the other, make peace between them. If either of them commits aggression against the other, fight against the aggressors till they submit to Allah's judgement. When they submit make peace between them in equity and justice; Allah loves those who act in justice."[2]

This text reminds us of the tendency of most religions to speak of their own kind without working through what their own kind have in common with outsiders and what is peculiar to them, what makes them distinctive. The assumption is that believers, fellow Muslims, should not be fighting. What they hold in common as believers ought to make fighting about temporal matters such as territory or national dignity ludicrous. Obviously this insight has not prevented Muslims from splattering their history with blood. The recent war between Iran and Iraq is a case in point. Equally obviously, Muslims have not been unique in their internecine battles. The recent strife between Protestants and Catholics in Northern Ireland is a case in point. Certainly, both the war between Iran and Iraq and the strife between Protestants and Catholics in Northern Ireland have more than religious causes. Economic, historical, and cultural differences all play strong roles. Equally obviously, however, the religious values the two parties hold in common, which to outsiders seem momentous, have not proven strong enough to keep them from killing one another. Like the European wars that followed on the sixteenth century Christian reformations, these more recent struggles have condemned both sides as not knowing how their God calls them to peace.

In this text the Qur'an is emphatic that believers should not be at one another's throats and that when they are others ought to separate them. The supposition seems to be that one or the other is likely to break the peace such separation would establish, or to refuse to stop attacking the other, so that the peacemakers will be forced to move against (fight with) the recalcitrant. This suggests that the Qur'an is not opposed to aggression or violence per se. No doctrinaire lauding of *ahimsa* makes violence catch in the Muslim's throat. Rather the peacemakers ought to beat on the aggressors until the aggressors see sense and submit to the judgment of Allah. How this judgment will be rendered is not explained. Presumably those who hold power in the Muslim community will pass sentence, assigning merits and demerits, blame and responsibility to make recompense, as the facts seem to warrant. However, the text is clear that if and when the parties submit to peace—the cessation of hostilities, arbitration of their grievances—they should receive fair-dealing. The authorities charged with overseeing the peace-process ought to assure both sides equity and justice.

The last line is the most winning: Allah loves those who act in justice. Like the talmudic rabbis concerned to render judgment with the utmost rectitude, Muhammad and those who glossed this text of the Qur'an had a vision of God as the font of fairness, equity, righteousness. But that Allah should love those who act in justice is remarkable, on the order of the confession of Krishna that the devotee is dear to him. True, Allah throughout is a more personal deity than the typical Hindu divinity and love is not far from compassion and mercy. Nonetheless, the typical Qur'anic view of Allah emphasizes the divine Lordship. The will of Allah carries its own persuasiveness, so there is no need to assure Muslims that Allah loves them. Yet assure them this text certainly does. If they will do what is right—here, lay down their arms and make peace—the Lord of the Worlds will look kindly upon them, will want to take them in his arms.

The text leaves in abeyance the question whether it is permitted to take up arms against unbelievers, but we know from other sources that in certain circumstances it is. The thought therefore occurs, how can all of us who are party to today's global culture, our increasingly interdependent world, overcome the distinction between insider and outsider that keeps us from applying such sentiments as these about infra-Muslim fighting to any human conflict? If it is unseemly for Muslims to be battling Muslims, Christians to be battling Christians, Jews to be battling Jews, what changes to make it seemly for Muslims to be battling Jews, Christians to be battling Muslims? All three groups believe there is only one God. All three grant the other two rights under that God, acknowledge ways in which the other two also are God's children. Can they, we, be so foolish as to think one can make such grants and still countenance bloody battling? Has *jihad* or crusade any future once one has correlated the one God and the one world?

We think it does not, and that until the Abrahamic traditions overcome their sense of chosenness, separateness, they will continue to betray the God who has summoned them. The psychology of chosenness and holy war is not hard to fathom: by radically distinguishing "us" from "them," we give ourselves a sharper identity, make our lives more intense, and exempt ourselves from recognizing that most of our claims to superiority or uniqueness are fatuous. This has long been obvious in Christian circles, but the ecumenical movement has brought it into clearer relief. The only significant reason the Christian churches have not reunited is their having come to love their particular identities more than the catholicity of the Christian Church as a whole. Such particular identities, honed through centuries of doctrinal and military battles, mean more to them than the prayer of Christ (John 17) that they be one. Naturally, outsiders perceive this to be a scandal, a stumbling block to professing Christian faith, as do sensitive insiders. Naturally, there are ugly analogies in the split between Shiite and Sunni Muslims, between Orthodox and Reformed Jews, and between different Hindu or Buddhist groups. Again and again the part loves partiality more than wholeness. Again and again the divine call to peace and neighborly love is dismissed as irrelevant, insipid, compared to the rush of excitement, the bloodlusty thrill, one gets when battling for one's own kind against the dirty outsider.

Ah, but what of the claims of all partial groups that they must in conscience cling to the truth as they see it and fight with tooth and nail what they perceive to be the godless error of those (whether within their own religious family or outside it) with whom they are at odds? Existentially, one of course has to follow one's conscience as formed at any given instance. In greater detachment, such a claim usually is unimpressive if not a downright insult to the intelligence. The "truths" that separate the various Christian churches are minuscule aspects of the catholic Christian faith, compared to the profession of the centrality of Jesus incumbent on all who choose the Christian way. Similarly, what Shiite and Sunni Muslims hold in common mocks their differences as irrelevant in the best of times and tools of Satan in times of war. Moreover, it is not hard to position all three Abrahamic religions as holding more in common than they hold apart. The members of all three are simply people, whose lives are short, who themselves have never seen God. The humility and common cause this ought to arouse brand the continuing hatreds among members of the Abrahamic faiths sheer stupidity. How could any of them really have known and loved the Lord, their God, and thought that Lord wanted them to slaughter the other as an infidel? Historically, the Muslims racing out to *ji-*

had and the Christian crusaders have been the greatest idiots, but nowadays we find hawks in all three traditions defacing their faiths. If Allah loves those who act in justice and wants peace between warring Muslims; if Adonai is longsuffering and abounding in steadfast love; if the Father of Jesus makes his sun to shine and his rain to fall on just and unjust alike; then any interpretation of the covenant, the Kingdom of God, or the seal of prophecy that tries to justify slaughtering others as a work of God is not just bogus but diabolical: a form of mental disease bespeaking the sin against the Holy Spirit, a deep if not utter separation from the divine will.

24:35–36/212: LIGHT

"Allah is the light of the heavens and the earth. His light may be compared to a niche that enshrines a lamp, the lamp within a crystal of star-like brightness. It is lit from a blessed olive tree neither eastern nor western. Its very oil would almost shine forth, though no fire touched it. Light upon light; Allah guides to His light whom He will."

This is a famous Qur'anic text, from which the whole of surah 24 has gotten its traditional name. And while light certainly is a common religious symbol, working in most traditions' sense of conversion, coming to realization (enlightenment), God's work in people's consciences, and the divine station in the heavens as the creator of the sun, the moon, the stars, and all under them, it has a special force in the Qur'an. Perhaps because Muhammad was formed by the desert, where light and darkness are dramatic, where the sun blazes down and little else fills the horizon, the light of Allah seems both especially intense and a fine symbol of the divine transcendence.

The divine transcendence and lordship have both physical and moral dimensions. Allah is the sole creator, the one from whom everything that has breath or even form derives. To "associate" anything with God would be to try to mar the divine transcendence, to cloud the uniqueness of the sole deity. That is why Muslims regard idolatry as the cardinal sin, and why lack of belief often is equated with idolatry. Similarly, that is why Islam prohibits representations of God, art that would try to humanize the deity or give it incarnational forms. No, Allah is the sole light, the sole source of definition and significance. He alone illumines the being, the purpose, of the heavens or the earth. And, as the imagery of our passage suggests, the light of Allah is wholly self-generated. Nothing outside of Allah sparks his flame, increases or diminishes his light. His light is but an expression of his essence and self. To be Allah is to be blazing truth, utter illumination, with no admixture of lies, ignorance, or darkness.

This furnishes Islam its grounds for making Allah the light of conscience as well as the light of the natural world. The creation over which Allah is Lord extends into people's souls. And just as Allah transcends the physical creation he illumines, being its source but infinite whether he creates it or not, so Allah transcends, goes far beyond, the moral light shining in the most saintly life. The holiness of Allah is only hinted by the holiness of the saints, just as the fullness of being Allah enjoys is only hinted by the splendors of the natural world. Further, the holiness, the good conscience, of the saints derives from the light and strength Allah has infused. Their prayers have taken them into communion with Allah, that he might transform their consciences. Their ascetical practices have opened them to the divine light. The saints who glow with the physical force (*barakah*) of Allah's inspiration suggest how light floods the personality open to God, becoming a psychosomatic aura. The Prophet, who enjoyed the fullest measures of divine light ever bestowed on a human being, revealed the practical wisdom such light can produce. His teaching, example, military leadership, and governance of the

Muslim community all depended on and reflected the light of Allah. The Qur'an of Allah given through him is the place the devout go to find the light their minds crave, the illumination proper to mature Muslims.

The last line of our text is intriguing. Allah guides to His light whom He will—inclusively or exclusively? Does the text mean that all light—truth, shining conscience, beauty shining in nature—comes from Allah, so that wherever one finds a good person or a beautiful scene one ought to call it a presence of Allah? Or does the text mean that Allah predestines sanctity and sinfulness, faith and unbelief, writing a script that invites some into the Garden and consigns others to the Fire? Islam has tended to straddle these two options, accepting both. The qualifications it has put on the inclusive, universalist reading boil down to a caution not to devalue Qur'anic revelation by making it seem indifferent whether people become truthful and good through Islam or some other tradition. Little in the Qur'an itself favors such an interpretation, for throughout Muhammad is convinced of the surpassing, nonpareil wonder of the revelation given him. The qualifications most Muslim theologians have put on the second, exclusive reading have boiled down to insisting that sufficient human freedom remains to hold individuals accountable for their deeds (and for whether they end up in the Garden or the Fire). Still, the sovereignty of Allah, blazing over the Muslim world like the sun blazing over the desert sands, has given Islam a strong appreciation of providence. Nothing escapes the foresight of Allah, nothing occurs unless Allah wills or agrees. One could speak of predestination, but Muslim theologians were well aware of the differences between the divine and the human modes of knowing, so such speech did not necessitate agreeing that Allah had mapped out ahead of time everything that later would occur. In Allah there is no ahead of time, no later or before, none of the discreteness unavoidable in finite, material beings. Just as one could never understand the divine being, so one could never understand the divine knowing and planning. The light of Allah was transcendent in the sense of too full for dim human minds ever to comprehend.

The Qur'anic view of the divine light suggests much of the problem devout Muslims have with modern approaches to culture, including modern approaches to peace and justice. By and large modern approaches are secular, relying on the light of human reason to guide them. Islam respects human reason but accounts it paltry compared to the illumination offered in the Qur'an. The case is quite parallel to Jews and Christians overwhelmed by the light of the Bible. Yet biblical criticism has developed into a respectable, accepted enterprise, while critical study of the Qur'an is at best in its adolescence, the majority of Muslims still being little influenced by it.

Textual criticism naturally becomes a delicate business when it is a matter of applying human light to scriptures believed to be repositories of divine light. Until people accept the fact that even religious scriptures have had human authors and editors, who have inevitably been constrained by the grammar and vocabulary of the language in which they were working, by the range of images operating in their culture, by the historical and scientific information available in their time, it will be hard to convince them that critical studies of scriptural texts are useful. As well, it will be hard to furnish them the safeguards reason offers against fanatics' interpreting scriptural passages as supporting bloody vengeance, misogynism, and a host of other things that enlightened people now consider evil.

So the light of Allah, transcendent though it be, would to some extent come into the keeping of critical Muslims, just as the biblical light, equally transcendent for Jews and Christians, has to some extent come into the keeping of critical Christians and Jews. Following the light of conscience has left many Christians and Jews no other choice than to distinguish among the many dicta of scripture, to discriminate some as fully wise, others as problematic. What about rendering justice to the poor, whether they be members of one's religious community or outsiders? What about granting other members of one's pluralistic culture equal civil rights? What about going to war over religious differences, or considering all who oppose one's religious policies minions of Satan? Can these policies be deduced from the scriptures as implied in the light of revelation? When one comes across people who hold them, is one encountering people whom Allah has guided to the light, or people whose own darkness has misguided them? Can people claim to be enlightened by God but in fact be dim, ignorant, ungodly?

50:5/119: GOD'S NEARNESS

"*We* created man. We know the promptings of his soul, and we are closer to them than the vein of his neck."

Here we have the classical text assuring Muslims that God is not only transcedent to creation but immanent within creation. If the being and light of Allah totally surpass human understanding, this does not mean God is far away, always over the river and through the woods. The fullness of divine being allows Allah to be as radically close as he is radically far. He is a part of human being, though of course he is not contained by human being. The pulse throbbing in one's throat is a sign of his nearness. The divine being is like the blood coursing through one's veins, like the air filling one's lungs, like the light that accompanies all one's thought. One could no more exaggerate the divine nearness than one could exaggerate the divine transcendence. Each is total, radical, complete. But because each is an attribute of God, the Perfect One, neither negates the other. God is not a game of x's and o's, a "place" where if one thing is true its polar opposite cannot be true.

God contains within himself all perfections, all possibilities. So God is both far and near, both other and close, both understanding and never to be understood.

The mystics of Islam exploited the nearness of God when they developed techniques for taking the soul along the stations to perfection. Occasionally one of them crossed the line of prudence and claimed full union, indeed identity, with God, which brought stern punishment (Al Hallaj was killed for such a claim), but as long as they maintained the Creator/creature distinction and despised idolatry they were free to promote awareness of the nearness of God. Nearness, after all, seemed to betoken intimacy. A Rab'ia, free of many inhibitions because she had been just a poor servant girl and craved no public notice, gave subsequent Sufis a model of passionate desire for intimacy with God. Her ideal was a love pure enough to want nothing for itself, but on the way to such a love she treated Allah as a lover and made the mystical quest a romance.

What light does the nearness of Allah shed on Islamic notions of peace and justice? First, it explains why Islam has wanted culture to be whole, a fusion of what modern Western cultures have divided between church and state. If God is present everywhere, nothing is profane, unrelated to God. Everything ought to come under God's sway, and insofar as God has made human beings the executives of his sway (starting with Muhammad and continuing with the caliphs who succeeded him) the leaders of the Islamic community hold jurisdiction over both political and religious matters.

Similarly, the mullahs—religious teachers—have felt free to concern themselves with education, home life, health care, and many other matters which in modern Western cultures would be considered the province of the secular state. They have felt free to interest themselves in war, and their recent numbers in Iran have included some interested in whipping up hatred against their country's enemies. It has mattered little whether such enemies had offended by secular or religious acts. As long as they had opposed the holistic Iranian culture, they had made themselves haters of God.

If we analyze such holism, we are drawn into the intriguing matter of the profits and losses exacted by modernity. The losses, brilliantly clear to the leaders of traditional Muslim regimes, include unrest, profanity, and lasciviousness. The somewhat mythic description of what used to be, favored by such leaders, includes law and order, based on the people's commonly accepting guidelines of Qur'anic *shariah (law)*. By distinguishing culture into two realms, the religious and the secular, modern Western democracies have cut the moorings that used to keep people anchored, content that they knew their place in the scheme of things, both cosmic and cultural. As well, people used to feel the world pulsing with holy energy, used to believe that the Allah as near as their pulse throbbed everywhere. Nothing was profane, cast outside the pale of the mosque. Everything was meaningful, right, dignified. So, for instance, the traditional roles of men and women seemed fitted into the order of creation. Islam was not so detailed about this instinct as India was when it elaborated caste, but in a general way Islam thought men and women had been made by God to occupy different yet complementary spheres. Each sphere was sacred. Neither men nor women had to agitate for their dignity.

Third, and obviously relatedly, the lewdness traditional Muslims see in contemporary Western cultures shocks them. Obviously, they think, this is what happens when one throws off old ways and allows people the freedom to pursue whatever they desire. The veiling of women, which was on the wane forty years ago, has revived, not simply because the male leaders of traditionalist regimes have commanded it but also because women wanting to associate themselves with Islamic faith and deploring the exploitation of women that occurs in liberated societies have freely donned it. Certainly, what one group calls exploitation another may call freedom. Progressive Muslim women might consider sexual advances a small price to pay for higher education and work in such professions as accounting, engineering, medicine. Traditionalist Muslim women might consider their exclusion from the circles holding religio-political power a small price to pay for the sense of dignity and order their traditional roles of being wife and mother have afforded. And the traditionalists would have the stronger claim to be living as the Qur'an prescribed, to be following the old, long-hallowed ways. The progressives would have to argue that their freedom was implicit in the Qur'an and that Muhammad would be pleased with their adaptation of Qur'anic principles to new situations.

There is no uninterpreted view of either tradition or present times. The nearness of Allah, at one's carotid and in one's soul, does not exempt one from having to make judgments and choices. Probably this is the strongest argument in the progressive armory. Modern thought has uncovered features of social consciousness that seem to apply always and everywhere. Always and everywhere, people have been making their social world by talking about it. They have talked with others, muttering agreement or disagreement about perceptions of fittingness and impropriety. They have talked with themselves, creating a constant stream of interior observations, questions, judgments that largely firmed up the foundations of what the consensus of their people considered reality but occasionally chipped at the edges. This has been true even when the main work of cultural construction has been interpreting a scripture such as the Qur'an. Traditional exegetes may have thought they were simply exposing the manifest sense of the text, as they may have thought the Qur'an had come down from heaven whole, entire, seamlessly weaving divine light into a heavenly Arabic. But we know better. Always their judgments about *jihad,* almsgiving, the pilgrimage, the inheritance rights of women, and the rest were acts of their own, shaped by their personalities and times, subject to a dozen pressures and sources of prejudice. On the other hand, traditionalists know better than moderns the chasm to which an unbridled use of this truth about the human, social construction of reality leads. The chasm is the possibility that there is no objective meaning, world, holiness. The chasm is the likelihood there is no revelation, nothing standing over-against the so manifestly inadequate human reason to correct and save it. In the measure one finds this likelihood horrible, one will be sympathetic to the holistic impulses of traditional religion. In the measure one thinks peace and justice have to be aspects of cultural wholeness, one will try hard to correlate reason and revelation, human competence and a global mystery human beings will never master. Similarly, in the measure one sees the totalitarian, repressive dangers in revelational traditions one will urge such correlation, such connection-yet-distinction, from the underside, the below of human consciousness. In the measure one finds religious revelations to have been used to sanction murders, wars of conquest, the subjugation of foreigners and women, the veto of humanistic research, and dozens of other trends enlightened reason finds anathema, one will beg both humanists and traditionalists to collaborate on a new image, a healthier ideal: the religious humanist who thinks truth and revelation compatible, peace and religious ardor compatible, doing justice the first requirement of the immanent holy God.

56:1,3/108: JUDGMENT AND PEACE

"When that which is coming comes—and no soul shall then deny its coming—some shall be abased and others exalted ... There they shall hear no idle talk, no sinful speech, but only the greeting, 'Peace! Peace!' "

The theme is judgment, a theme dear to Muhammad's early preaching and maintained throughout the Qur'an. Like the eschatological sections of the synoptic gospels and the early letters of Paul, the expectation is that judgment will be rendered soon. Muhammad, like Plato, used judgment to give his teachings a trans-secular foundation. What he was proposing as justice and wisdom went to the depths of reality, went into the Godhead, and so could never make sense to sensual, secular people. Their horizon was limited to the utilitarian, to what might profit them during their brief earthly span. Muhammad was reporting a revelation from Allah, with whom nothing was earthly or brief. For Muhammad ultimate prosperity was being blessed by Allah and ultimate ruin was being cursed by Allah. No earthly wealth, reputation, or power was worth a penny compared to the treasure of Allah's approval. The only sensible, rational life was to live so as to please Allah and be among the blessed on Judgment Day.

On Judgment Day, the blessed would hear the customary greeting—Peace!—not as a routinized, familiar salutation but as a thing of wondrous force. With Allah there would be full peace, the joy and fulfillment of the Garden. Reaching out to such a consummation, so devoutly to be wished, the souls of the blessed, the just, would be free of this-worldly entanglements. Nothing this-worldly could threaten them to the bedrock, just as nothing this-worldly could thrill them. They were free. Indeed, only they were truly free. All worldlings, all people who invested in material success or fame, were enslaved to perishable goals bound to give them nightmares.

This is the dimension of Islam, and of religion generally, that secular modernity finds incomprehensible. By its dogma that life ends with the grave, much modern thought has closed the door to the perennial philosophy nourished in the great religious traditions. As well, it has truncated anthropology, the sense of what human nature is and can amount to. So it tends to write Islam and its sister faiths off as hopelessly irrational, if not dangerously fanatical. By the same token, it attempts to develop a political science guided only by this-worldly, empirical experiences and certitudes. The result, in the eyes of

165

the traditional religions, is something spastic, disordered, bound to bring pain.

Take the notion of Hobbes that fear of death is the predominant human passion and so the lever to political control. Take the proposition of Machiavelli that people voluntarily give up their yearnings for heaven, because that will make them better citizens. Both express a belief that "heaven," "judgment," "immortality," and the rest are chimerical, illusory. Both miss the deep symbolic function of such images, which has been to preserve an open soul. Without these symbols, and their Eastern equivalents ("moksha," "nirvana"), human beings would seem the prey of threats to bodily harm, would be unbearably tempted to agree that might makes right. These symbols have stood against such pragmatism, such ignobility. In the ironic splendor of their helplessness, their apparent insubstantiality, they have proven stronger than the military divisions those trying to conquer by physical might have arrayed. Human beings will not live by depravity alone. They will not accept anthropologies that deny the outreach of the inmost parts of themselves. They have been made for heaven, Allah, the Tao, the Kingdom of Heaven, the World to Come. Even when they have little understanding of how such terms function in their souls, they sense that secularism is a prison, a place where the lights would go out and the most important, beautiful aspect of being human would vanish.

Witness the ugliness of present-day high fashion, the ugliness of the art in totalitarian regimes, the insubstantial, unnourishing character of most popular literature and music. Because they have not been created in the grip of an eros for the transcendent, they have not touched the soul and mobilized its deepest energies. Muslim architecture stands as an interesting contrast. What stories have been to Jewish culture and music has been to Christian culture, architecture has been in Islam. The most famous mosques bespeak souls formed by the transcendence of Allah. One cannot fabricate such a formation. One cannot hide the fact that one's own creations

166

have come from a spirit limited to this-worldly horizons. The peace that secular architecture brings seldom approaches the peace insinuated by a great mosque, or by a Zen garden, or by any of the Masses of the great Christian composers. It is like trying to play on a little four-stringed zither while your counterpart has a twelve-stringed guitar. It is like being limited to a baby violin while your counterpart has access to a cello.

Muhammad does not use these contrasts, largely because he had no modern secularism standing over-against him. But he does take aim at the practical atheists of his day, and he does imply that they will never know the full reaches of peace. Because he had no doubts that Allah was completely real, demanded justice, and would right the wrongs of this world in his own domain, Muhammad thought ignoring Allah was the greatest of follies. One simply could not know the measure of human being, nature, or possibility if one did not set all one's data and judgments in the framework of the primal Islamic confession: There is no God but God, and Muhammad is His Prophet. At Judgment Day, that confession would be the resonant theme-song. Those who had taken it to heart, made it their own anthem, would be blessed and overflowing with peace. Those who had ignored it, rejected it, deemed it a loony tune would weep and despair, thoroughly chastened by God's reality.

Does this suggest we will not have justice and peace until most people accept the reality of God and interpret their yearnings as a hunger for God's splendor? It does indeed. But the suggestion need not flower in only Muslim, Christian, or any other religious forms. It can flower in people put off by the self-serving and fanaticism of the religions. It can work in hearts that do not feel at home in any of the established traditions. What it has to produce anywhere, though, is a practical awareness that integrity, the ethical life, is a function of mysticism, understood as a sense that the realest things are beyond our grasp. Such a sense could degenerate into occultism, but the mysticism we have in mind is much simpler,

167

more sober, humbler. In ordinary times it amounts to suffering the outreach, the longings of our spirit for a peace that surpasses understanding, a justice human regimes never accomplish. In traumatic times, it amounts to sacrificing advantage, reputation, in the limit case even life for the sake of maintaining the conviction that our intimations of immortality are the most significant thing about us. When people die for their faith in God, they usually depend not on catechetical formulas but on such a conviction seared in their souls. They cannot deny God because God has been the relational other stimulating their most precious thoughts and hopes: a truth uncorrupted, friends never failing, a love worthy of one's best, creations that will escape death, a redemption of innocent suffering, a justification for bringing children into the world, a vindication of Muhammad, Jesus, Moses, Lao Tzu and all the others who have touched all our souls, given us joy, routed despair and made time a march toward otherworldly beauty.

2:172/335: PRAYER AND ALMS

"Attend to your prayers and pay the alms-tax. Your good works shall be rewarded by Allah. He is watching over all your actions."

The great foundation of Islamic spirituality is the Qur'an.[3] Verses like these have formed both lawyers and Sufis, both the learned who pored over the text and the illiterate who heard it recited in the mosque. Here we come upon a pithy dyad: pray and give for the support of the poor. Let us first reflect on its two injunctions and then consider the rewards of Allah the overseer.

Most religious traditions, if not most cultures generally, have sensed that a full human life, a mature personality, balances contemplation and action. Certainly there have been innumerable disputes over which ought to take priority, but few cultures have disputed the need for both. Thus China, as we have seen, developed Confucianism to care for the office and Taoism to care for retirement. Thus Buddhism balanced morality, ethical action, with meditation and studies of wisdom. Christianity had its symbolism of Mary and Martha. Judaism balanced Torah with good deeds and marriage. Here Islam is pitching in with its agreement. On the one hand, one must attend to the prayers stipulated for five times each day, that Allah may be properly praised and one's soul be properly fed. On the other hand, one must do something to improve the world, fulfill one's social responsibilities, hoist part of the burden of the widow, the orphan, the suffering.

The danger in contemplation is to become purely theoretical, concerned only with ideas or love of God. Taken too far, Taoist retirement leaves the world in the hands of dullards, fools, knaves. The danger in action is forgetting the needs of the soul, the primacy of God, the call to love the divine mystery with full mind, heart, soul and strength. Thus Hinduism offered the active the discipline of karma-yoga, lest their work be riddled by desire and so immerse them more deeply in the tar-pit of karma. Thus Confucianism stressed benevolence and ritual—forms to give action heart and grace. Islam has known times when its spirituality became so otherworldly that its culture had little creativity. Then art, science, jurisprudence, and philosophy all faltered. Then ignorance, illiteracy, and superstition thrived. On the other hand, it has seen military and religious adventures little disciplined by deep prayer, careening out of control for lack of mystical counterbalance. In such failures to achieve a golden mean it of course has joined Christianity, Judaism, and all the other religious traditions. Fourteenth century Latin Christendom was in terrible disarray, in good part because plague and papal corruption had taken away people's heart, leaving them disinterested in the incarnational side of their faith and culture, inclining them either to brood morbidly or lose themselves in carnal excesses. Modern Judaism has had difficulty keeping its contemplative rabbis friendly with its social activists. Often the two have split, producing many secular Jews scornful of messianism and easy pickings for Marxism-Leninism.

The prayer that would properly counterbalance activist excesses administers peace like a benign medication. Lost in God, the divine mystery, the spirit gives over the ambitions and fears that tend to make action misguided or excessive. The action that would keep contemplation from becoming quietistic stays close to actual people and their actual needs. Most important among such people are the poor, in whose lives God's goodness may be hard to see, and the suffering, who challenge the joys of contemplation. For its ordinary folk, Islam has legislated the five-fold daily prayer, which like the Christian rosary tends to be as profound or shallow as the person using it. The five-fold daily prayer itself is simply an occasion, a form. What one puts into it is one's own affair. If used wisely, as an effective instance of the Muslim virtue of "remembrance" (of God, Judgment Day, one's reason for being on earth), the daily prayer can become a beloved discipline, something one performs the way one eats or washes: for nourishment and pleasure, for cleansing and renewal.

The same with the alms all Muslims have been expected to contribute. Obviously one could do more than the minimum, contributing beyond the two percent or so of one's income that has been the rough expectation. And, equally obviously, one could extend the notion of almsgiving to include charity of other sorts: visiting the sick, easing their discomforts, looking out for the orphan, helping the ignorant, sharing one's surplus food and clothing. But whatever one did, the alms, like the pilgrimage to Mecca, recalled the solidarity of the Muslim community. The way of Allah was not solipsistic. The deepest contemplation had made Muhammad more political and social-minded, not less. The joys of one Muslim ought to be the joys of all, as the sufferings of one Muslim ought to be the sufferings of all.

170

The good works of prayer and almsgiving ascend to Allah like the scent of a pleasing sacrifice. He will reward those who follow his will in both the contemplative and active dimensions of their lives. Islam does not preach a doctrine of salvation by faith alone. It does not think human beings are so sunk in sin they can do nothing to please Allah. Allah, their Creator, has given freedom sufficient to hold them responsible for their having prayed or not prayed, helped the unfortunate or not helped them. Their deeds are more important than their intentions. The road to the Fire is paved with good intentions. Unless they have heeded the cry of the beggars, "Alms for the love of Allah," they will have little defense on Judgment Day. Unless they have heeded the call to prayer, they will stand as practical atheists. And, to adapt a New Testament saying, Muslim religious teachers realized that only those who do the truth come to the light. Contemplation directs one to action, but action has a reciprocal influence on contemplation. If one has never sacrificed for one's Qur'anic faith, one is not likely to grasp its profundity. If one has never identified with the poor and the suffering, one's protestations of charity will seem academic.

Allah watches over all of our efforts to learn these truths, embody them, work out our salvation in fear and trembling. The lives of human beings are open to heaven. What we think hidden is patent to God. So there is no fooling the depths of one's being, where Allah is as near as the light by which one examines one's conscience. There is no interpreting away the twofold imperative of praying and giving alms, loving God and doing something practical to help one's neighbors. The right ring these injunctions have in the religious conscience is a hint from Allah. The appeal they have for many secularists hints that the soul frequently belies the acquisitive lifestyle, the narcissism urged by the slick magazines.

With regular contemplation, one learns the proportions of peace: God is more important than one's career, the spirit is more important than the body. God and the spirit properly

171

reverenced can make one's career a vocation and the body a sacrament. With regular alms-giving one learns the proportions of justice: we have rightful claims on one another, the goods of the earth are for all the earth's people, if one sees a brother or sister in need and does not give what help one can one is a hypocrite to be claiming to love God, whom one cannot see. A great task remains (translating these soul-truths into effective public policies), but the Qur'anic dyad suggests the way forward. And, Allah is watching.

Discussion Questions

1. How adequate or comprehensive a religious program is that summarized in the five pillars?

2. Why has Islam so castigated idolatry?

3. How does Allah regard strife within the Muslim community?

4. How valid are most religious schisms?

5. Why is the transcendence of God a source of human freedom?

6. How can a misunderstanding of transcendence lead to fanaticism?

7. What can the modern mind make of the claim that Allah is as near as the pulse at one's throat?

8. How might the nearness of Allah inspire a whole, healthy culture?

9. How ought Judgment Day to function in the healthy religious psyche?

10. What has Judgment Day to do with this-worldly peace and justice?

11. Why is contemplation not a waste of time?

12. How could alms-giving epitomize compassion and proper social action?

Notes

1. For general background on Islam, see Fazlur Rahman *et al.,* "Islam," ER, vol. 7, pp. 303–453; Cyril Glasse, *Concise Encyclopedia of Islam* (Atlantic Highlands, N.J.: Humanities Press Internation, 1986); Ismail and Lois al Faruqi, *The Cultural Atlas of Islam* (New York: Macmillan, 1986); W. Montgomery Watt, *Muhammad: Prophet and Statesman* (New York: Oxford University Press, 1974); Marshall G.S. Hodgson, *The Venture of Islam* (Chicago: University of Chicago Press, 1974); Kenneth Cragg, *The House of Islam* (Encino, Calif.: Dickenson, 1975); *Islam: Muhammad and His Religion,* ed. Arthur Jeffrey (New York: Bobbs-Merrill, 1975); *The Cambridge History of Islam,* ed. P. M. Holt *et al.* (Cambridge: University Press, 1970); Annemarie Schimmel, *Mystical Dimensions of Islam* (Chapel Hill: University of North Carolina Press, 1975); Clifford Geertz, *Islam Observed* (Chicago: University of Chicago Press, 1971); Frederick Mathewson Denny, *An Introduction to Islam* (New York: Macmillan, 1985); *Women in Contemporary Muslim Societies,* ed. Jane I. Smith (Lewisburgh, Penn.: Bucknell University Press, 1980), and V. I. Naipaul, *Among the Believers* (New York: Vintage, 1982).

2. All translations are from N.J. Dawood, *The Koran,* 3rd. rev. ed. (Baltimore: Penguin, 1968). Indications of specific verses within the sura cited are approximate(*) because Dawood does not give a running enumeration. The last number in the citation gives the page in Dawood where the quotation occurs.

3. On Islamic spirituality see *Islamic Spirituality: Foundations,* ed. Seyyed Hossein Nasr (New York: Crossroad, 1987).

Chapter 8

CONCLUSION

THE SELF AND POLITICAL SCIENCE

The scriptures of the world religions place more emphasis on the self than on political, economic, or sociological factors. This is in part because they come from a pre-modern time, when social science as we now know it had not developed. It is in part because they stem from a time when the level of technological development did not allow people to contemplate greatly altering the cycles of nature or programming the social interactions of human beings. However, probably the main reason the scriptures of the world religions address the individual human person is their assumption and conviction that each person is a free, responsible agent, able to alter his or her sense of God, self, the world, and fellow human beings. The scriptures are interested in meaning, which is a function of personal consciousness (as well as social consensus). Get people to dwell within a new meaning, convert them to the worldview announced by the scripture, and you would have changed their lives as significantly as if you had given them a new nationality, sex, or set of senses.

The fascinating, maddening fact of human existence that bedevils work for peace and justice, as well as all other sorts of work, is the dialectic between the one of the unique human being and the many of human groups (states, churches, nations, miscellaneous organizations, and so forth). The scriptures certainly are aware of the many, but they tend to concentrate on the one, even when they address a group such as the Muslim "believers." The assumption is that the Gita, the Dhammapada, the Analects, the Tao Te Ching, the Talmud, the Qur'an is being heard by people who vary in their circumstances, sufferings, intelligence, needs yet are alike in their suitability for the general message of the scripture in question. For example, the Gita uses Arjuna as an everyman, whose questions about war and action have analogues in all people's lives sufficient to make Krishna's teachings about yoga, detachment, bhakti and the rest always relevant. Thus the oneness, the uniqueness, of the individuals the Gita has in mind does not inhibit it from laying out general principles. The Gita, like the Dhammapada, thinks that detachment would help any human being improve karma, lessen suffering, get better perspective on the objective order, on wisdom and peace.

What the scriptures do not do is take social groups as concrete sensoria of God. By this we mean that the scriptures all think that God or ultimate reality works in people as individuals, being present to each human conscience, mind, and heart. When one speaks of "the people," "the state," or "the church," one is speaking at a higher level of abstraction. All three of these terms name realities, things actually functioning, but they are not the primary object of conversion, inspiration, mystical experience, and the other ways the divine Spirit changes people's lives. Any person of course is greatly shaped by the education, information, and manipulation that come through the impact of other people. But for the scriptures of the world religions none of this social influence determines how the person will respond to the direct initiative of God. As well, none of it comes from the inrush of ultimate reality into the heart or conscience of a social group. A social group does not have a heart or a conscience, except by pale analogy to the individuals who compose it. Saying this does not mean saying that people are isolated monads, living sealed off from one another. Obviously, that is not the case. But the more fully people mature in their religion, the more their ideas of the divine mystery clarify and deepen, the less they are prisoners of public opinion, the less they are swept away by social contagion.

On the other hand, the more fully people mature in their religion, they more fit they are to join with other people in profound, loving relationships. Communities, in contrast to herdlike groups, come from free, mature individuals and in turn further their freedom and maturity. So we are not saying that people grow in isolation, nor that isolation is the human ideal. Far from it. But we are saying that the individual human conscience is the only fully concrete place where the divine presence is sensed and works. Only God is more intimate to people than they are to themselves, working their transformation into the divine image and likeness. And the only images and likenesses of the divine mystery, the only concrete, fully real instances of potential buddhanature, are specific individuals. Therefore, a great deal of socio-political talk (Marxist, Liberal, Facist alike) is deluded. Because it speaks as though groups were the primordial realities and individuals were derivative, it misses the mark and fails to grasp the actual dynamics of conversion.

We have drawn this conviction, and many other theses about political reality, from the work of Eric Voegelin.[1] The great experience behind Voegelin's political science was the rise of Nazism in Germany and Austria in the 1930s, which he witnessed at first hand. From that experience Voegelin derived a life-long skepticism of mass movements and what he called "gnostic" worldviews. Such worldviews forget the primacy of the individual and fail to comprehend the actual span of human consciousness (awareness, and so meaning). They neglect the material foundations of human life, the ties with nature that we cannot sever. Equally, they forget or fail to recognize our tension toward the divine ground of existence—how the divine mystery lures us, how we are always trying to transcend the limits of our present constellation of meanings and gain something more comprehensive. So they dismiss such basic phenomena as death, finitude, and ignorance (to say nothing of sin), which ought to tutor human beings from below—from the fundament of the earth. The elementary facts about us human beings, crucial in any estimate of how we ought to live together, include our mortality, our physical and spiritual limitations, all the ways in which we are not God or the Dharmakaya (cosmic body of the Buddha). These elementary facts, discernible in each human life, ought to inculcate a bedrock humility and sense of humor. The first thing to be said about any of us is that he or she is not God—does not know it all, is not going to be around very long in the cosmic scheme of things, ought to be pitied for the weakness epitomized in having vulnerable, breakable human flesh. Any political philosophy that neglects these bedrock truths and rides roughshod over people is bound to be a bad servant.

On the other hand, any political philosophy that neglects the transcendent outreach of the human spirit is equally pernicious. The second part of the equation, which an adequate political philosophy balances with the implications of our debts to matter, is our being lured by the Brahman, the Buddhanature, the Tao, Adonai, Allah. If we are not pure angels, pure intellects, we also are not pure beasts, all matter. We want to know and love unrestrictedly. We feel stirrings of immortality, passions for a light and warmth physical nature cannot give. Much of our meaning comes from such stirrings, so we cannot be well-defined apart from them. Equally, we will not be well-served until we enjoy a political philosophy and regime that treasure us as ends rather than means, that labor to provide us the opportunity to move into God through contemplation—art, science, social service, worship, romance, and any of the other human activities that cry out, "We are good in our own right and ought to be done for our own sakes."

A balanced political philosophy produces justice and peace by squaring with what people actually are. It serves up, for all citizens, bread and roses. It tries to ward off, for all citizens, war, unemployment, hunger, illiteracy, boredom, destruction through error, drugs, triviality, pornography. The self deserves bread and roses, because the self is an embodied spirit. War, unemployment, and the rest cripple the self and so render community difficult, sometimes even impossible. The beginnings of peace and justice lie in an adequate political anthropology—in a view of who we are that opens out what we have to do if we are to live together sanely, creatively, happily.

CONVERSION AND ORDER

Without denying that the scriptures we have treated vary considerably in their views, we would argue that they share a thorough acknowledgement of both the material and the transcendent aspects of human nature. In other words, they share a healthy consciousness, one not deformed by the schizophrenia apparent in such phenomena as Nazism, Stalinism, Maoism, and Capitalist materialism. Each such ism, to be sure, begs precise clarifications. For our purposes, however, they are sufficient simply to suggest the major ways in which modern political philosophies have become so deformed they have thought massive slaughter or a flight from the divine mystery a way of health. The delusions of a Hitler, a Stalin, a Mao would be laughable, had not rivers of blood run in their wake. The materialism of the affluent West would be laughable, were it not issuing in shrunken souls, drugged out bodies and minds, and were there not standing over-against it, like furies soon to become avengers, the wretched of the earth, with their bloated bodies and their depressed, venegeful souls.

The scriptures we have treated sing in harmony that human beings are not the measure that gives order. To be human, we have to open ourselves to the divine more, to the mystery that is trans-human. We may call this the Tao that cannot be named, or the Way of the ancients. We may symbolize it by Krishna or the Buddha. Or we may forbid all representations of it, as we call it Allah or Adonai. Whatever, when we follow the traditions of the world's great scriptures our naming, symbolizing, and forbidding will be in the service of a balanced, ordered worldview by contrast with which modernity seems diseased. Once again, a full treatment of these issues would require many qualifications: problems with the scriptures, ways in which modernity generated more differentiation and truth (for example, about history and the place of symbols in human consciousness, about repression and slavery), ways in which right order and so health have continued to live in individuals, despite the disease of their modern cultures. Nonetheless, because the scriptures stand duty for cultural ideals that balanced mortality and immortality, fidelity to the earth and fidelity to heaven, as ours have not, they give us criteria against which we can test our modern selves, to see what is wanting (which turns out to be: why there is so much strife and injustice in our time).

A conversion is a shift of perspective, a change of mind and heart, the forsaking of old gods for a new God. In our usage here, it is leaving disorder to embrace order, leaving idols to let the divine mystery take over in the shrine of one's soul. When converted, rightly ordered, we can look death in the face and neither frolic nor despair. When converted, we can find traces of divinity everywhere, perhaps most winningly in the silence of midnight, the twilight of our idols, the pauses in the dark night of the spirit when no-thing-ness becomes delicious. Converted people acclaim the golden rule, because their ordered souls recognize other human beings as their essential equals. They do not do unto others what they themselves find hateful, because they feel others to be of the same flesh as themselves and of the same family of God. Of course, even the converted are imperfect. Often they do not keep faith with the order shown them by the divine mystery. Often they neglect the golden rule, preferring the superficial-

179

ity of lawyers' codes. Like the rest of us, they find it hard to bear the divine mystery, which sometimes is frightening, a maker of deserts. Still, they overcome these imperfections through a love of order, a fellow-feeling, that makes them insightful, sympathetic, and realistic. The realistic assessment of human beings is that they are both mortal and immortal, both warped and wonderful, bound to hurt you but likely to treat you better than you deserve. You need to hold them to their commitments, without forgetting that mercy is more important than sacrifice. You should expect to suffer from their follies, to have yourself to sacrifice, and yet to realize occasionally that everything is grace—existence you neither made nor merited.

We shall deal with evil in the next section. Here the topic is conversion and order: the shifts that show what is independently of us and what therefore should tutor our subjective consciousness. Nature is, independently of us, and even though we assault nature brutally it continues to outlive us, dwarf us, project a silence that embarrasses our chatter and would make our return to the earth a gentle embrace. Other people are, independently of us, and their variety, contrariness, beauty and ugliness defeat both our solipsism and our tidy political schemes. We are, independently of ourselves, since we did not bring ourselves into being and, failing suicide, we will not take ourselves out of being. Our bodies don't fully obey us, do immense amounts of work we don't appreciate, allow us to reproduce our kind without guaranteeing the next generation will improve on our sorry performance. Our minds are wonderful yet fallible, clear yet biased, apparently busy and full yet more deeply quiet, waiting, and blank. Our hearts are sweet and sour, clear and muddy, restless until they rest in the divine mystery, until they give themselves to the divine Other. We can do little about all this otherness, this ineluctable objectivity, except suffer it.

And God is, despite all our ignorance, sin, distraction, repudiation. We cannot kill God, although we can make deadly, diseased cultures. God is the horizon without which we have no thought. God is the creativity without which there is no nature. The silence of God is the condition of our speech. The speech of God brings the silence, and ideally the obedience, of our talky minds. God is not a thing, and so God cannot disappear. We cannot talk about God, name God, love God into submission. We can only acknowledge, not run away, let God love us into submission. At the bend of our minds, where the corner of infinity appears, the peace and justice of God glimmer. We can never get around that bend, yet only by heading toward it can we fly a straight course. Thinking about God ensnares us in such hopeless paradoxes. Yet God remains, endures, stands by, waiting for us to let go of ordinary thinking, to realize that the divine mystery orders us from within, bubbling up like an underground spring, showing us we float over an abyss that is also a pleroma, a fullness pledged not to let us down.

Floating over the abyss that is a pleroma, we are free of the ties that make war and dominating others attractive. What is money, when seen from the abyss? What is military power, political clout, peer applause? As Lao Tzu might put it, what seems most obscure turns out to be most revelatory. What seems most mystical, inward, retired turns out to be most realistic, objective, and creative at the office. Turn from trivia, ephemera, the strife of people seeking advantage and you find the profound, the lasting, the peaceful. It is not wholly formless, because it blows through the ten thousand things and makes nature signs of its Lordship. It is not dull because it quickens the poets, the lovers, the people of prayer. It is not impotent because it originally moved the mountains to their places and since then has stabilized the great resisters, those who have kept saying no to the dementia and violence. It is near as the pulse at our throats. It offers instruction, Torah, through hundreds of shamans, prophets and sages.

If none of this description makes any sense, you need more time with the religious classics. If none of it deflates the reality of Wall Street, the Pentagon, Capitol Hill, you need more time with the quiet of your own soul. And if none of it is encouraging, freeing, we have spoken badly. For in itself the Tao is the loveliest no-thing in our midst, the Qur'an is liberation from the worst bondage. Of course the faithful, the orthodox, the priests and pundits besmirch divinity and make faith difficult, but in the end even they can't ward off the inevitable. Inevitably, people stumble into a time of peace, or feel a spasm of outrage, that levels all human authority. Inevitably, they turn at least 90 degrees toward right order and for a moment wonder, dream, of what going 90 more could do for the world. In their half-turn, they feel a wind at their side that could be the divine Spirit. Once felt, it need only be remembered, refelt, allowed to polish the golden rule. Then the glow of peace and justice begins to angle around the bend and we know where we have to go, to what we have to be converted.

SPIRITUALITY AND STRUCTURAL CHANGE

Among the places to which we have to go, "spirituality" now comes to mind. Among the things to which we have to be converted, "structural change" now comes to mind. We would have "spirituality" connote love of the divine mystery that enhances one's love of the earth and reknits the bones of selfhood fractured by Enlightenment criticism. We would have "structural change" connote the practical follow-through spirituality implies for politics, economics, and social relations. Certainly one could summon other terms. What concerns us is not the name but the reality. As long as other terms were faithful to the twofoldness of human existence—heavenly and earthly, solitary and communitarian—we would not protest. The twofoldness, of course, ideally is a unified range of being. It is not two halves awkwardly glued together, stone and wood factitiously joined. William H. Poteat's neologism, "mindbodily," renders much of the incarnational ideal we have in mind.[2] All of us stem from the divine mystery. In our unity, our sinews-cum-soul, we live through the Platonic in-between, supported by matter and lured by divine spirit.

Spirituality has many good, nourishing actions regarding which it can claim both parenthood and descent. It begets art, science, romance, and political protest, while these in turn educate it for its next developments. The least ambiguous spiritual act, however, is religious contemplation. Fronting the ungraspable divine mystery, the human spirit realizes it has come upon the limit of limits, the border that defines what "human" has to mean. In earlier cultures, this limit often was not differentiated from "nature." Nature was the great matrix from which all things issued and unto which all things returned. But with the noetic differentiations of Greece and the pneumatic differentiations of Israel, the philosophers and prophets clarified the properties of divinity as such. Unlike nature, divinity as such was not representable. It was not a thing but the source of the being of all things. The primary wonder in the philosophers' world was that one could predicate of a thing, "It is, it exists." The primary wonder in the prophets' world was, "That which is sovereignly has established personal relations with us." Either way, in Greek or Hebrew categories, the measure for human beings, the source of human order, presented itself for contemplation and obedience. Thus Aristotle made the contemplative life the acme of human activities, while the prophets made the love of God, the new covenant written in the heart, the wellspring of social justice. If one wanted to decode the symbols praised by the philosophers, one had to catch the traces of the Thought that thought itself. If one wanted to understand the Torah, one had to listen to the Shema, really hear how Israel was formed by relation to a Lord that was only One, could have no equal among the nations. In a word, one was riveted to contemplation: recall of one's beginnings in the Exodus, remembrance of the divine drawing of one's spirit up toward the vision of the Good.

The Eastern analogues certainly were just that—likenesses with significant differences—but they all counseled contemplation with equal force. Hindu yoga, Buddhist meditation, Taoist reflection, and Confucian study were so many different variations on the same theme: set your mind and heart on the source, the creative mystery. One could not become a significant Hindu, Buddhist, Taoist, or Confucian without forsaking the superficial realms, the zones of gossip and unreflective tradition. One had to go back to the sources, plumb one's own spirit, learn what Dharma and Tao originally had meant. The reverberations of that original naming got stronger as one left facile, superficial speech and descended to the wellsprings. One could recapture something of the originating experience. Indeed, the Dharma and Tao, not being of human manufacture, in themselves were as vital, as burnished, as they had ever been. Like the Torah and the Qur'an, they came from a heaven where worm could not enter to destroy, where moth found neither window nor fustian.

The structural changes implied by reattuning the self to the divine measure would be far more radical than most professional politicians, economists, and educators would consider feasible. Indeed, they make little sense until one has come into the grip of the spirituality we have sketched and found it a new creation. For example, one thinks of the Pauline insight (Galatians 3:28): neither Jew nor Gentile, neither slave nor free, neither male nor female. Beneath all the distinctions, differences, reasons for estrangement and hatred, Paul saw something more significant that all Christians held in common. We can leave for another day the complicated matter of how one best translates such commonality for a religiously plural world in which there seem to be many paths to salvation.[3] In the simple terms that our reflections on the scriptures of the world religions have developed, it might well be the sameness of desire and heart assumed by the golden rule.

In the glow of this sameness, think of political rights— how valuable the perceptions and hopes of the founders of the

American experiment were, and how far their project has fallen short (of its intrinsic goals, which stretch far beyond the practical politics they probably envisioned). Were there no Jew or Greek—no discrimination based on nationality, race, or religion; no prejudice that made "Russian" or "Oriental" the conjurer of a bestial foe—we would lose half the impetus for our arms races. Were there no slave or free—no overlords and underlyings, no egregiously rich or poor—we would lose another forty percent. Were there no male or female, no disputes about the equal humanity of women and men, domestic peace and justice might become an anchor and base-line securing the nations' political, military, economic, and cultural fair-dealing.

But if even the Christian churches have failed the Pauline vision, as even the religious establishments of Israel and Islam, India and China, have failed the vision of their saints, how can one hope to form structures worthy of the divine mystery, able to embody the order revealed through spiritual exercises? This is a mild yet basic form of the problem of evil. Many people barely glimpse right order, while most of those who have seen it naked end their lives confessing they never acted upon it wholeheartedly. The vast majority of us are living, but only partially, seeing, but through a very dark glass. What, then, are we to do?

We are to try, beating back the voices and images that say it is useless, foolish, to think God willing (if able) to do something for us. We are to let go—of our preference for scenes that cannot abide the divine mystery, that are incompatible with judging human beings more like than different, more equal under heaven than distinguished. We are to realize we can make a difference, all the while that we reckon such difference likely to be small. We are to make sure that peace and justice prevail where we do have influence: in our hearts, in our homes. We are not to keep such light under a bushel but to act upon it publicly, doing unto others in public both what we want them to do unto us and what we would do unto them privately, were there no pressure from the unjust, the unfair, the violent to keep up the old antagonisms. And, most of all, we are to act on our convictions enough to have them disciplined, toughened, made realistic. They need to be stripped of the aestheticism and conceit they easily accrue when kept merely matters for contemplation. Only practice will perfect them. Only those who do the truth will come to the light, although even those who try to do the truth and fail come home the better for it. Even those who end feeling they have but half begun learn about the divine mystery, the one thing necessary for anyone's justification and peace.

There is no understanding the reality of evil. It is absurd through and through. But we can battle it, and when the divine mystery shows itself a love that suffers evil with us, fighting at our side, we can redeem our lives from the evil pit—as all the great scriptures have promised.

Discussion Questions

1. Why is the self the only fully concrete sensorium of the divine transcendence?

2. How do political propaganda and consumerist advertising try to deny the primacy of both God's address to individuals and the community such address would build?

3. To what should one try to be converted?

4. How is conversion likely to occur?

5. How do spiritual exercises create a political vision at odds with war and domination?

6. What does Galatians 3:28 need by way of supplement if we are to have social structures worthy of the divine mystery?

Notes

1. See Eric Voegelin, *Anamnesis* (Notre Dame, Ind.: University of Notre Dame Press, 1978).

2. See William H. Poteat, *Polanyian Meditations* (Durham, N.C.: Duke University Press, 1985).

3. See *The Myth of Christian Uniqueness,* ed. Paul F. Knitter and John Hicks (Maryknoll, N.Y.: Orbis, 1988).

NAME INDEX

Arjuna, 20–33 *passim*, 37, 102, 175; *See also* Krishna, *Bhagavad-Gita*

Augustine, St., 53

Barth, Karl, 14

Brown, Robert McAfee, 53

Confucius (Master Kung): background of, 70–78; and Aristotle, 86–89; and Plato, 86; *See also Analects*, Confucianism

Fingarette, Herbert, 71–72, 95

Gandhi, Mahatma, 14, 40, 57, 58

Gautama, 44, 58, 65

Haughton, Rosemary, 3–4, 15–16

Hillel, R., 134, 135

Jnanananda, Ma, 38–39

King, Martin Luther, Jr., 40

Krishna, 20–24 *passim*, 26–27, 29, 33, 37, 40–41, 153, 179; *See also* Arjuna, *Bhagavad-Gita*

Lao Tzu, 72, 96, 98–99, 102, 104–105, 109, 110, 168, 181; See also *Tao Te Ching*, Taoism

Lonergan, Bernard, 14

Muhammad, background of, 148–51; See also *Qur'an*, Islam

Newman, John Cardinal, 12–13

Niebuhr, Reinhold, power of grace, 10–11

Rahner, Karl, 4, 14, 16, 135

Rahula, Walpola, 46, 56, 68, 69

Shammai, 134

Tutu, Desmond, 40

Voegelin, Eric, 176–77

Wiesel, Elie, 14, 40

SUBJECT INDEX

Analects: description of, 12, 74–76; teachings of, 74–95
anger, Buddhist perspective, 52–56
atman, and Brahman, 44–45

Bhagavad-Gita: description of, 11, 12, 19–42, 175; *See also* Krishna, Arjuna
bhakti, 19, 37
Bodhisattvas, 46–47
Brahman, explained, 44–45, 64–66
Buddhism: description of, 44–68; See also *Dhammapada*

caste system: explained, 26; Buddhist perspective, 47, 64
classics: definition of, 11, 13; examples of, 12ff.; purpose and importance of, 14, 78–79
Confucianism: overview of, 70–95; contrasted with Taoism, 96–97, 100, 108, 110, 115, 169

contemplative, contemplation, described, 39–41, 169

demonic: Hindu perspective, 33–37; *See also* evil
detachment: Buddhist, 53–56, 127, Christian, 32; Judaic, 127
Dhammapada: description of, 11–14, 48–49, 175; teachings of, 48–68
Dharma ("teaching" and "duty"): explained, 19–20, 26; and Buddhism, 45–46, 47, 49, 60, 184
dialogue, contemporary interreligious, 7–11, 32–33, 154–56
divinity: Buddhist perspective, 62, 106; Hindu perspective, 29–33, 37–38; Muslim (Islamic) perspective, 156–64; Taoist perspective, 106, 117; and St. Thomas Aquinas, 106; general overview of, 180–81

189